# DRAWBRIDGE BRITAIN

First published in 2018
by Eyewear Publishing Ltd
Suite 333, 19-21 Crawford Street
London, W1H 1PJ
United Kingdom

*Graphic design by* Edwin Smet
*Cover image by* Getty (West Indian Arrivals, by Haywood Magee)
*Author photograph by* Ingrid Abreu Scherer
*Printed in England by* TJ International Ltd, Padstow, Cornwall

Set in Bembo 13,3 / 17 pt
ISBN 978-1-912477-79-1


WWW.EYEWEARPUBLISHING.COM

# DRAWBRIDGE BRITAIN:

## LOVE AND HOSTILITY IN IMMIGRATION POLICY FROM WINDRUSH TO THE PRESENT

# RUSSELL HARGRAVE

 **EYEWEAR** PUBLISHING

SQUINT
BOOKS

Dr Russell Hargrave is a freelance reporter. His work has appeared in *The Guardian* and *Public Finance*, and on ITV News and Reuters. He writes regularly on immigration and international development for politics.co.uk and devex.com.

Hargrave is also a policy advisor to the Liberal Democrats on immigration and refugees.

*Drawbridge Britain* is his first book.

# PREFACE

## A migrant story

In August 2017 a friend at ITV News asked me to help her out on a story.

It was two months after the disaster at Grenfell Tower in west London. More than seventy people had lost their lives in the two-hundred-foot block of council flats in the early hours of 14th June, when a fire started by a faulty fridge freezer blazed out of control, trapping people on the upper floors.

Britain woke to scenes which could have come from a horror movie. The video footage is still shocking: blue and orange flames lapped through the building, luminous against the black night. The fire smouldered on for two and a half days.

Grenfell Tower sat, poor and largely forgotten by the powers-that-be, in Kensington, one of the richest boroughs in one of the world's wealthiest cities. A home half a mile away in trendy Notting Hill would set you back £1.5 million.

Grenfell residents may have been able to see these grand town houses, but they lived in another world. This was a home for the poor and the forgotten, and especially for immigrant families originally from the middle east and north Africa. Their tower had no sprinkler system, defective fire extinguishers, and only one internal fire escape. Residents had written and blogged about these dangers but were ignored. It soon emerged that the tower's external walls were clad with combustible tiles, after the council had rejected a more expensive, fire-resistant alternative.[1]

The combustible cladding meant that when tenants followed the official advice on what to do in the event of a fire – to stay in their homes and wait for help because the blaze would not spread from flat to flat – they were condemned to death. *The New York Times*, looking on from the other side of the world, called the tragedy 'a somber monument to inequality.'[2]

It left a shattered community behind. After a night punctuated by emergency vehicles and the screams of trapped residents, thousands of people needed trauma counselling. More than two hundred households were homeless, and children were returning to classrooms where some desks were suddenly sitting empty.

As so often amid tragedy, the Grenfell fire inspired extraordinary generosity from the British public. Within days a shocked nation had donated £18 million to look after survivors. This was the story my friend was interested in. How much of that money had been spent and where had it gone?

But I didn't find the story I expected.

The public's money was being distributed to nearly a hundred local charities. My job was to phone each one and try to draw together a picture of how all this cash was being used to help traumatised survivors.[3]

What I found was a series of tiny local groups using very thin resources to look after a patchwork of poor immigrant communities across Grenfell: the Somali Development Organization, the Eritrean Women's Empowerment Group, the Persian Care Centre, the Sudanese Association, the Al-Hasiniya Moroccan Women's Project. The list went on. Many of these charities had just a few hundred pounds in the bank. They were run from front rooms, by people working in their second or third language, offering support to migrants who had landed in this plot of west London from every corner of the globe. I talked with people who had lived in the tower and people who had known victims of the fire. Some sounded like they were still in shock.

The charities made it clear: the people they helped were resilient, but there were few formal resources for learning English; jobs were pretty scarce; and what jobs did exist were precarious and poorly paid. The relationship between residents and the local council, strained even before the fire, had broken down completely. The support network for survivors came instead from one another and from these tiny charities, which had existed for years by scraping together what money they could. The influx of donations was welcome but it wasn't going to undo years of neglect.

I hadn't realised it until I started making those phone calls, but bubbling away under the Grenfell tragedy was another story. In the midst of poverty and political failure, Britain today is a tough place for many immigrants.

Imagine this as a spectrum. At the extreme end is Grenfell, where families new to Britain had been repeatedly let down by the state, thrown into a poor corner of the capital city and relegated to unsafe housing, largely forgotten even by the council supposedly looking after them. They would probably have remained forgotten to the outside world had tragedy not struck. But as we move along the spectrum, so we find the historical moments which have, in small and large measures, cranked-up pressure on immigrants in Britain. Political demagogues demanding that they pack up and leave. Screaming headlines about immigrants lying and scrounging. Legislation designed to humiliate them.

This is the history *Drawbridge Britain* will tell. It will look at how Britain has been changed by immigration (and how Britain has changed immigrants); how successive governments have tried to make the country a 'hostile environment' for migrants, long before that phrase was adopted by today's politicians; and how a sceptical but decent British public has, for the most part, tried to find a way to build a future with their new neighbours.

## 'All social ills'

To illustrate what I mean when I say Britain can be tough for immigrants, here are a few brief facts, picked more or less at random from recent years.

A tabloid reporter in 2013 described the editorial angle of the newspaper where he worked. 'It is very much the cartoon baddy,' he said, 'the caricature, you know, all social ills can be traced to immigrants and asylum seekers flowing into the country.'[4]

Or this: the government has spent half a billion pounds in the last four years on high-security immigration detention centres. Prisons in all but name, their sole purpose is to lock up immigrants as if they are criminals. Dozens of people have died in immigration detention during the last decade, yet the conditions there remain shrouded in secrecy.[5]

Or: a committee of MPs heard about the abuse suffered by immigrant children in Britain, and reported 'eggs thrown at houses, stones thrown at babies and children hounded from school.'[6]

Or: in one 2014 poll, Britain was second only to Greece, the country right on the frontline of this decade's migrant crisis, among western voters who believed there were 'too many immigrants in our country.'[7]

This is just a snapshot. There are plenty more where these came from.

## A sceptical island

On the face of it, this doesn't make much sense at all. Why do the authorities, the press and the public take such a dim view of immigration when the evidence shows overwhelmingly that it is good for Britain?

Immigrants have boosted the national economy by about £20 billion in recent years (enough to pay for three million hip operations). They pay more in taxes than they ever take out in welfare. The bits of England which host the most immigrants also see more entrepreneurship and more start-up small businesses, which in turn take on more local staff. Government data on community cohesion shows that, after decades of growing immigration, people are happier in their neighbourhoods than ever before.[8]

I will cheerfully lay my cards on the table. I believe immigration is good. Forcing it down artificially is bad for the economy and will make life culturally poorer in ways we will regret. Immigration is a dynamic process and I like the things it brings: new faces, new languages, new ideas, new rhythms to a place.

But I am in a minority, and if you agree with me then you are too. Britain is an island of immigration sceptics. For as long as pollsters have asked questions about immigration, the majority of the public have said that it is too high and that they want to see it come down, regardless of how many people are actually coming into the country at any given time.[9]

Within this majority are a small but noisy collection of out-and-out racists and xenophobes (around a tenth of the population today, according to one think tank estimate)[10] as well as people unhappy about immigration and swayed to stronger feelings by political panic and media scare stories.

Most people worry about immigration for more mundane reasons, though. They belong to what I would call the 'sceptical middle', a great big chunk of the public we will think about more in the last section of this book. There is nothing extreme about their views on immigration. They care about society around them and want Britain to be a decent and welcoming place, but they are nervous about how that society may be changing. Those new languages and rhythms which I find dynamic can also seem disruptive and chaotic. Modern life is messy and sometimes immigration gets the blame: the views formed during the school run and down the pub will always trump abstract government statistics about national wealth and happiness. The British Social Attitudes Survey in 2017 summed-up this view neatly: 'the public has not typically been enthusiastic about immigration, but they have shown a degree of pragmatism about it.'[11] The former Conservative minister Stephen Green says Britain has 'demonstrated a far-from-perfect, but nonetheless relatively easy-going, openness to the world at large.'[12] These both seem pretty sensible. We aren't a nation of angry extremists but of worriers, grumpy about immigration but pragmatic about finding ways to get on with our lives regardless.

This book will talk a lot about integration as one way to do this, so it useful to agree a definition. Integration is a slippery concept but I understand it as a sort of deal, whereby newcomers contribute to society and share its values and laws and are wholly entitled to expect decency and fairness in return. When I use the term, this is what I mean.

## A history of modern Britain

*Drawbridge Britain* will move, roughly chronologically, from the arrival of four hundred British citizens from the West Indies aboard the HMS *Windrush* at Tilbury Docks in 1948 up to the present day and the aftermath of the vote for Brexit in 2016. I admit that this is a slightly arbitrary starting point, but the *Windrush* is an iconic moment in several ways.

Firstly, its arrival marked the beginning of a sudden, sustained period of immigration, and the first real questioning of whether Britain, still labouring under delusions of imperial power, should keep her borders open to the world. The *Windrush* made this question more urgent, by heralding the start of a sudden, dramatic growth in the number of people moving to these shores. The first thousand West Indians made the voyage during 1948, selling property and possessions to fund what would have been an uncertain venture. By 1956 the route to Britain was well established, and that year 46,000 people made the same crossing. People from all over the globe headed to Britain after the war, but the *Windrush* and the boats which followed were remarkable for the public and political attention they received. This drew other questions into focus: how much immigration was too much? Should Britain welcome workers; and if so, what about their families? What about refugees fleeing violence in other countries? Should the government get involved in integrating new communities or leave people to get on with it? It was also a question of identity: immediately after the war most migrants were also British citizens, so did Britain have any right to close the border to them? This book will look at all these things.

Secondly, the *Windrush* and her successors provoked a strong and fascinating public reaction, as people responded to their new neighbours with a mix of welcome, bafflement and horror. Thirdly, it led to a speech which remains one of the most famous (or infamous) political moments of the last seventy years: Enoch Powell and his 'Rivers of Blood,' a speech which reverberates to this day. And fourthly, it was *Windrush* families who, years later, were robbed of their liberty, jobs and healthcare through Theresa May's own cruel immigration policies. This sorry, scandalous tale is told in chapter four.

The *Windrush* also feels the right place to start because the chain of events – sudden movements of people, unpredictable public reactions, and political panic – is a pattern we will see again and again as we move through the narrative of modern immigration to Britain. We will see it in the way husbands and wives were allowed to join their families here only to be humiliated and demeaned when they chose to do so, and in the way the country tried to honour its commitment to refugees only to accuse the same people of being ungrateful and dishonest. The hostile environment may only have become official government policy in 2015, but as an approach to immigration it began decades earlier.

## Omissions

We will look at foreign labourers, students, husbands and wives, stowaways, refugees, and the myriad other categories into which migrants fall. I concede that there is more on refugees than you might find in other books about immigration, something which reflects my own background working with asylum seekers. But whatever the category, all these lives could easily fill a book many times longer than this one.

This means there are plenty of things which won't be covered in the pages ahead. This isn't a complete history of the period, nor does it pretend to be. It is more like a *Selected Poems* than a *Collected Works*, if you like. It tries to knit together a series of key moments in immigration to Britain in recent years, to tell a coherent story about what this meant for the country and the people arriving here.

Inevitably, there are omissions. We will hear the stories of many immigrants to Britain, but I haven't conducted in-depth original interviews with people trying to find their feet here. For readers interested in stories of this kind, *Finding Home*, by the journalist Emily Dugan, is a wonderful book. The ten personal journeys Dugan traces, of immigrants trying to navigate 'the tug of two homes... the slog of work and the pain of separation from those they love,' are patiently and beautifully told.[13]

Neither will this book try to cover the many centuries of immigration which occurred before the 40s. This isn't to suggest for a moment that I think the only immigration stories worth telling began after the war. There are many excellent sources of information on the rich history which helped shape modern Britain. I recommend two books in particular: Robert Winder's exhaustive *Bloody Foreigners* and David Olusoga's *Black and British*. The latter is full of compelling details, including the harrowing discovery that the *Windrush* has its own history, as a vessel belonging to the Third Reich, used to transport Jews across Scandinavia from where the majority were murdered in concentration camps.

Similarly, the recent bloody conflicts and persecution which have driven people to Britain as refugees deserve more attention than I can offer here. I have largely limited myself to what happened once people reached British soil. Again, there are numerous superb books and articles for those who want to fill in the gaps. As an overview, Samantha Power's *'A Problem from Hell'* is the most compelling account of how individual lives can be disrupted, uprooted and destroyed by the forces of civil war and violence.

It is also an uplifting reminder of human courage and the (often very ordinary) people who stand up against evil.

Finally, I make no claim that this is the last word on what modern immigration means to Britain. We should always share our opinions more rather than less, especially on a topic which some claim (wrongly) hasn't been discussed openly or enough. Whether you believe immigration is a boost to British culture or slowly killing the country – whether the topic fills you with feelings of love or feelings of hostility – it's good to talk.

Many personal experiences are drawn from my time as an MP's caseworker, a unique environment for seeing how immigration policy impacts on people's lives. Data is taken from the Oxford Migration Observatory unless otherwise stated, an impressive, independent source of stats and numbers. Chapter three, on the treatment of refugees in modern Britain, revisits some topics I first wrote about in my report *Dividing Lines*, published by the charity Asylum Aid in 2014; chapter four, on Theresa May, expands ideas from my contribution to *Tactical Reading*, a collection of essays published by Eyewear Publishing just before the snap General Election in 2017.

# INTRODUCTION
# IMMIGRATION MATTERS

## Brexit questions

Every story must start somewhere. This one starts in the same place it ends: Brexit.

'I was just so sad,' says Pauline Bock, a French journalist living in London, about the morning of 24th June 2016. She sounds exhausted just remembering it. 'I really didn't recognise the country.'[14]

Bock was one of the three million EU citizens in Britain whose lives had just been plunged into uncertainty. The country had voted in a referendum to leave the European Union, changing completely our relationship with our closest neighbours. After a bruising campaign, voters turned out in their droves and the Brexiteers won with a clear 52% of the vote – and no one knew what was going to happen next.

What we *did* know pretty quickly, though, was that immigration was at the heart of their victory.

Indeed, we now know just how dominant immigration was as the driving force behind the Leave vote. Experts at the British Electoral Survey released data shortly after the referendum, generating a word cloud to show the answers given by voters on why they had backed Brexit (Figure 1). Immigration looms enormously over everything else. No other topic comes close.[15]

As the dust cleared, however, an awful lot of questions suddenly emerged into view. Not for the first time in the recent history of immigration, the reality was vastly more complex than politicians had claimed. Someone was going to have to come up with answers.

Most obviously, leaving the EU would mean ending free movement for European citizens to come to Britain to live, work and study. Some Leave voters were impatient to see this commitment honoured, so when were the borders closing?

Figure 1. Source: British Electoral Survey

In the meantime, the campaign had also seen Nigel Farage, the leader of the staunchly anti-European UK Independence Party (UKIP), unveil a poster in which a snaking queue of brown-skinned refugees waited at an unidentified European border. 'Breaking point,' screamed the poster. So was Brexit, as the poster implied, going to block people from *outside* Europe as well?

And there was more. Some leading Brexiteers had told ethnic-minority Brits during the campaign that ending free movement for Europeans would actually make it simpler for families to travel here from outside Europe.[16] It is easy to see why this was an attractive idea: why should British-Bangladeshis, say, watch their loved ones traipse through humiliating and expensive attempts to get visas to Britain when anyone from Europe could just waltz in?

But that idea directly contradicted the one unveiled by Farage. So which was it? When Britain left the EU, would immigration from outside Europe come down... or go up?

It quickly became clear that Brexiteers had no clear answers. One related issue did rise to prominence, though, one which seemed, at least at first glance, to be quite straightforward, and which would offer everyone in the country a chance to think about immigration and the Brexit vote. What would happen to the EU nationals currently living in Britain? How would we treat Pauline Bock and her millions of fellow Europeans living all over the country?

## Bargaining chips

To answer this, let's rewind a bit.

In 2004, ten new countries joined the European Union: Cyprus, the Czech Republic, Estonia, Hungary, Latvia, Lithuania, Malta, Poland, Slovakia, and Slovenia, collectively known as the A10. Under free movement rules, citizens of these countries were now free to live and work in any other EU country if they wished (although restrictions were already looser for Cyprus and Malta as members of the commonwealth). Large western European economies had the option to delay the process a bit while they prepared, an option taken up by Germany and France. Britain opened its borders immediately.

This was under Tony Blair's New Labour government, and the move had all the hallmarks of that era. It was bold and outward-looking, and it placed Britain at the political centre of a confident, modern Europe. At the same time, and equally typically of the era, it also paid scant attention to actual details.

The Home Office predicted that somewhere between 5,000 and 13,000 people would come to Britain each year from the A10 countries. This was so far wide of the mark as to be farcical.[17] 130,000 people had come by the end of 2005 alone, with hundreds of thousands more following each and every year after that, led by Polish workers and their families.

The British economy was booming, thanks, in part, to the contribution of all these European citizens. A decade on from opening the borders to the A10 countries, Europeans had spread out across the British economy, but there were areas where they made a particular impact: more than 300,000 EU nationals worked in manufacturing and in retail; more than 200,000 could be found on construction sites, working in hospitality, and delivering health and social care. [18] While some newcomers only ever planned to stay for a short while, many decided to put down roots. They bought homes and started families. The number of Europeans living in Britain shot up.

So did the political salience of immigration, and what the Oxford Migration Observatory calls 'the rise of immigration from a marginal concern to one of the few most-frequently named issues.' It wasn't that people suddenly started to worry about immigration, but that these worries rushed to the surface. Barely 5% of people named immigration as one of their main causes for concern in the 90s, but this had grown to 30-35% by around 2002, and then 40-45%

between 2006-08, rising back to those levels again from 2014 onward. Immigration had risen to record levels in this period as we shall see, both from Europe and further afield, and plenty of people were unhappy about it.[19]

By 2015, then Prime Minister David Cameron needed to stop his Conservative Party bleeding support to UKIP, which was campaigning effectively on the supposed excesses of European migration to Britain. Cameron's solution seemed rather neat at the time: pledge an in/out referendum on EU membership for after that year's General Election to settle the question once and for all, attack the Labour Party (who weren't offering a referendum), and then fight and win the campaign to stay in Europe.

Neat, with one obvious flaw. The promise did indeed put a brake on UKIP's progress and Labour were dispatched to defeat – but Cameron, heading up the Remain side, proceeded to lose the referendum.

By this time, an estimated three million European citizens were living in Britain, people who didn't have British passports but lived here as our neighbours, sending their kids to local schools and paying their taxes. Their lives had been thrown into chaos overnight, in a political gamble which had gone spectacularly wrong. The decent thing – surely the only defensible decision – would be to extend their right to stay. The government wouldn't pitch the lives of our European colleagues and friends into limbo – would it?

As things turned out, yes it would. In the weeks after the vote, ministers were repeatedly asked to confirm that European nationals would be allowed to stay. They refused every time to make any sort of pledge. International Trade Secretary Liam Fox even told the Conservative Party Conference in October 2016 that promising to let Europeans stay in Britain would 'hand over one of our main cards in the negotiations' over Brexit.[20] There was uproar at the idea that immigrants' lives could become bargaining chips, handy collateral in some grand game over Britain's future. But that is exactly what they were.

At the end of 2016, some European citizens received letters from the Home Office warning them, out of nowhere, that they could be deported. [21] The government insisted that these letters were sent in error, but European immigrants were suddenly, unmistakably living at the sharp end of Brexit talks.

Bock wrote that she had started carrying all the ID she could think of whenever she travelled, because she had no idea whether she might be detained coming in and out of the country.[22] People 'have built their family life in this country,' she said, 'and now fear they may lose it all overnight.'

'When I got back to France, people started asking me, *What about you? What about Brexit?* And month after month when I would go back to my parents and my family everybody would still be asking the same question, and my answer would be *I have no idea.*'

'A lot of people told me that they thought Cameron had a plan,' Bock says. 'But there was no plan.'

The idea of mass forced removals to mainland Europe might be fanciful, but officials let the threat hang in the air. The Polish family next door, or the German woman at the next desk, may look like neighbours and colleagues, but the government increasingly treated them as hostages.

Until suddenly, one day, they relented. In December 2017 the British government finally reached a deal on the first phase of Brexit, even if the details were vague. European citizens *could* stay in the land many called home. 'I greatly value the depth of the contribution you make – enriching every part of our economy, our society, our culture and our national life,' wrote Theresa May, Cameron's successor as Prime Minister, addressing European citizens directly on Facebook. 'You will have your rights written into UK law.'[23]

Except that if this was true in December then it had been just as true eighteen months earlier. It was a move typical of May (as we will see in chapter four): determined to appear tough on immigration, she was happy to leave EU immigrants living in limbo for as long as it was politically useful. She could have released three million people from that uncertainty at any point, but she did not. It was 2018 by the time the government finally cobbled together a system which would allow Europeans to register and stay in their homes.

The Prime Minister had shown her true colours to Europeans living, working and studying in Britain. It didn't go unnoticed.

## Leaving

In the first year after Brexit, EU citizens voted with their feet. The numbers from the Office for National Statistics are clear. More EU citizens left (123,000 in the twelve months after the vote, up around 30%), and fewer were moving the other way into Britain (that was down by around 20%). Although more Europeans were still arriving than leaving, the numbers had shifted significantly. EU citizens were leaving Britain in higher numbers than ever before, and the country had become less attractive to people looking in from the outside.[24]

'There's not one EU citizen who isn't thinking about it right now,' says Bock. 'It's not that they want to leave Britain. They still love the country, they still love their friends and this life. It is just that they don't trust the government anymore. They have seen a part of Britain that they didn't know or didn't want to know.'

## A short history

This book is a short history of how Britain did this to itself. The government opened our borders to immigrants and then, in a contradiction we will see over and over again, treated those immigrants with disdain and hostility. We will see how politicians let it happen, and the effect this had.

Until the second half of the twentieth century, Britain had few if any immigration controls. This was largely an effect of imperial confidence. Open borders allowed trade (and traders) to flow more easily across the empire, and let British administrators do their work unimpeded. The reciprocal right to cross British borders was extended to citizens of the colonies but this was largely theoretical, given the disparity of financial power and the fact that global movement was, compared with today, unimaginably complicated. This is not to say that Britain did not already have a thriving immigrant population before the war, but it is important to stress that open borders existing almost entirely for the benefit of British people and British profits, not outsiders.

Amid the collapse of empire and growing immigration from the commonwealth, politicians started to close that open border. Legislation in the 50s, 60s and 70s tightened significantly the rules on who could enter Britain. Even though immigration numbers would drop away again in the two decades that followed, public anxiety on the topic endured and the nation's politicians remained nervous.

Political confidence about immigration re-emerged in the 90s and 2000s. Borders were opened again (inside the European Union at least), and it became much easier to travel into Britain from other parts of the world, too. Millions of people took up the offer to be part of our island story – upon which political and popular opinion turned once again, and we became a more brittle and introverted nation as a result.

It was in this period that we started to hear all about 'immigration clampdowns,' a phrase politicians and journalists would soon be using a lot. Front pages screamed about the perils of immigrants, sometimes for weeks and months in a row. More legislation and rule-changes were rolled-out, designed either to stop people coming to Britain or to make life so miserable for immigrants already here that it put off others from joining them. The government had tried to make life harder for immigrants to Britain almost as soon as they started arriving in any great number, and by the early decades of the twenty-first century this 'hostile environment' was something ministers boasted about.

## One more book about immigration

There are quite a few books about British immigration. Some are good, some are rubbish. So why add this one to the pile? There are four broad arguments for writing this now.

### 1 Britain is home to a lot of immigrants

There are lots of immigrants living in Britain today (that is to say, to borrow the same definition used by the government, people who have lived here for at least twelve months but were born in a different country).

Numbers can be a cold way to approach millions of people's lives, but they also pack a powerful narrative punch. All those arrows on the evening news, or graphs climbing and falling: they tell their own story and we would be daft to ignore them.

In the vast period between the late Victorian era and the end of the twentieth century, people were more likely to be leaving Britain than coming here. The exception – for a stretch of the 50s and early 60s – provoked the first immigration panic of modern times, of which much more in chapters one and two. But for most years until 1993, immigration was actually holding population growth down. In technical terms, net migration to the UK was negative. In 1981, for example, 80,000 more people *left* Britain than came to live here, many of them Brits heading off to warmer climates elsewhere in the commonwealth.

Then it all changed.

From 1993, net migration started to rise. And it wasn't a question of a few hundred new arrivals. After 1997 in particular, thousands upon thousands of people were moving to Britain.

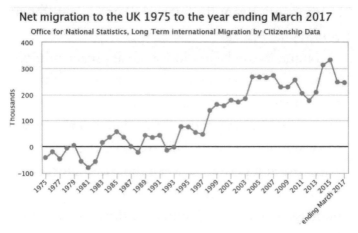

Figure 2. Source: Migration Watch

It is all there in Figure 2.[25] Net migration into Britain was 48,000 in 1997 and had jumped to 140,000 just a year later. By 2004 it was 268,000. In 2014 and 2015 it was over 300,000.

Immigration has added more than one million people to the population in the last four years alone. People from all over the globe have brought their own religions and cultures and languages. Douglas Murray, the most compelling anti-immigration writer around, argues that the speed and scale of recent immigration is something Britain hasn't seen before.[26] That is incontrovertible. Immigration has changed the country, and parts of Britain have been transformed in ways which would stun people of past generations. Some of us think this is great, many don't. But it has undoubtedly happened, and it is part of our story.

2 Brits talk about immigration non-stop (no matter what people claim)

Everyone has an opinion on immigration. In fact, if this book does nothing else it would be nice to nail the lie that no one is allowed to talk about it.

Here is Michael Howard, then the Conservative leader, speaking in the run-up to the General Election in 2005:

For too long immigration has been a taboo subject – however bad the situation has been, we've
not been allowed to talk about it. Well, I'm not
going to let the government sweep this under the
carpet anymore. Britain has reached a turning
point. We need to control and limit immigration.[27]

The idea that in 2005 people couldn't talk about
immigration – that even mentioning it was such a
'taboo' that normal folk dared not try – is rubbish.
People talked about immigration all the time, in
the pub and the corner shop, in church and in the
mosque (and a good thing too). Taxi drivers had a
ready supply of opinions on the issue, while radio
phone-ins invited contributions from anyone who
held them.

Plus it was a topic that sold newspapers by the
shedload. The *Daily Express*, towards the end of
2002, ran twenty-two separate front-page splash-
es about asylum seekers in a single month (in the
end it stopped only because its own staff begged
editors to give it a rest). This was when the power of newspapers to inform the public and set
the political agenda was still at its height. At
that time the *Express* sold just shy of a million
copies every day. Its great mid-market rival, the
*Daily Mail*, ran a vast number of asylum stories for
its own daily readership of two and a half million.[28]

Britain wasn't talking about immigration? Absolute dross. At the very moment that Howard got up to complain that it was a taboo subject, people were talking about it everywhere you looked.

Let's get real. We can talk about immigration and we do, just as we have for years. There is no secretly-enforced ban. People worried about immigration have been free to say so for years, just as people have been able to celebrate immigration if they wished. The guardians of political correctness, those guys who will come and shut you away for talking about immigration, don't exist.

The question is less whether the conversation happens than what it looks like. We need to find a way to make all this talk worthwhile. At its worst, it ends up with people on either side of the debate screaming past one another. This is how the historian Robert Winder describes the atmosphere in the mid-2000s:

> the [immigration] debate was unusually rancid and polarised. Both sides wrote and spoke as if they were in the minority. Little England correspondents poured scorn on the lily-livered pinkos who wanted to turn the country into a refugee camp, while the lily-livered pinkos themselves posed as brave moralists surrounded by a nation of thugs and morons.[29]

It is pointless and depressing to go through all that again. Hopefully this book can play one small part in finding another way.

## 3 Immigrants are under attack from politicians across the world

The past two or three years has seen a rightward, anti-migrant lurch across western politics, one which imperils immigrants all over the globe.

In common with so many depressing tales of today's politics, it involves Donald Trump. His election is a symbol of a nationalist fervour that goes far beyond the United States, a fervour he stoked in order to get elected. Trump knew the lurch was coming, as he propelled himself to the US presidency in 2016 using an anti-establishment shtick in which immigrants were centre stage, a scapegoat for problems real and imagined. Mexican migrants were 'drug dealers, criminals, rapists,' Trump proclaimed, just as he promised 'a total and complete shutdown of Muslims entering the United States'.[30] Within two years infant children were separated from their parents and put in cages on the US border, in the name of controlling immigration. The photos and audio of toddlers wailing in distress as they were taken from their families shook the world.

Nigel Farage knew the lurch was coming, too, as he unveiled that refugee poster during Brexit campaigning. And he is part of a list – a dizzyingly gloomy one – of politicians grown stronger off the back of xenophobia and racism.

The National Front in France, represented by Marie le Pen, talked of a Muslim 'occupation' of France, and later promised to stack the odds against new migrants and 'adopt favouritism across social services,' as the BBC drily put it.[31] Le Pen won more than ten million votes in the country's 2017 presidential run-off. She lost, but doubled the vote share her father had managed in 2002 (le Pen senior has been convicted six times for inciting racial hatred).

The Oxford-educated Prime Minister of Hungary, Viktor Orbán, reacted to the movement of migrants across mainland Europe by telling an international audience in 2016: 'For us, migration is not a solution but a problem... not medicine but poison, we don't need it and we won't swallow it.'[32] It bolstered Orban's position as the third longest-serving Prime Minister in his country's history. 'Hungary just didn't want migrants,' explained Heather Staff, an expert on the region.[33]

Alternative für Deutschland (AfD), Germany's right-wing populists, came third in their 2017 elections, but again the trend was a hefty move towards anti-immigrant sentiment. AfD enjoyed a swing of nearly 8%, while voters moved against Angela Merkel's ruling coalition. [34] Merkel won, but she had conceded serious ground to parties who made immigration concerns central to their campaigns. Across the border in Austria, the Nazi-inspired Freedom Party now controls national policy on, among other things, security and policing, thanks to a deal with the centre-right People's Party.[35] Matteo Salvini, a senior member of Italy's ruling populist coalition, called in 2017 for a 'mass cleansing, street by street' to clear migrants from Italian cities. It is chilling.[36]

There were some exceptions, not least here in Britain, where Jeremy Corbyn's Labour party, with its more laissez-faire approach to immigration control, made ground on Theresa May's much tougher Conservatives at the 2017 General Election. But in the main, progressive politicians face a crisis. Right-wing forces have been marshalled to fight election after election, and they are making major inroads across the western world.

A calmer, more balanced conversation about immigration isn't just a sensible thing to have, it is a political necessity.


## 4 Lying is making a comeback

Facts are under threat. Anyone who writes – anyone, for that matter, who takes the basics of democracy seriously – will worry about living in the 'post-truth' era. This is undoubtedly where we have ended up, another grim phenomenon ushered in by the election of Donald Trump.

Trump is a liar, an inveterate fibber from whom untruths pour forth apparently unstoppably. Trump's own lies on the campaign trail have followed him like a slime trail into the Oval Office. At the very moment that he levels accusations of 'fake news' against his enemies, he is up to his knees in his own fakery. Even his claims about giving away money to charity turned out to be false, and they set the standard for a presidency full of lies.[37]

But 'post-truth' doesn't simply mean that lies have replaced truth, like some Orwellian nightmare come true. It is even more sinister than that.

Truthfulness, as a concept, has been debased. The world's most powerful man, with his own disregard for telling the truth, has untethered his statements from reality. Using the biggest bully pulpit of all, the president of the United States pours scorn on any facts which contradict his chosen view of the world.

For Trump verifiable information, the very stuff of good policy-making, has been replaced with competing voices, white noise that he can listen to or not depending on what he wants to believe. 'In almost all the interviews, Mr. Trump's associates raised questions about his capacity and willingness to differentiate bad information from something that is true,' said one *New York Times* profile.[38] In other words, if the President hears something he doesn't like, he literally assumes it is untrue, and broadcasts that assumption to the entire world.

All those big concepts, of truth and trust and honour, have been hollowed out. And Britain is facing its own fight. 'People in this country have had enough of experts,' said Michael Gove famously during the Brexit campaign.[39] As Gove surely knew, take away a well-informed, decent debate and you are left with a free for all. Conspiracy theories have always enjoyed currency in immigration debates, and the post-truth era is just going to make them harder to shift. Ludicrous claims have gained credence merely through being repeated often enough: that the government gives money to charities teaching immigrant girls how to play hopscotch (the *Daily Mail* printed this nonsense back in 2011);[40] that asylum seekers once ate one of the queen's swans (from *The Sun* all the way back in 2003, a story we will encounter again in chapter three, and which has stuck in the shared imagination despite being fabricated);[41] that the government is hiding from us the 'true' population of Britain, which immigration has driven above 90 million (this drivel is only ever a few clicks away on Facebook); that asylum seekers get free council homes (they don't, but social media has swapped versions of this myth for years). There are many, many more.

This book will, hopefully, shift the debate about immigration onto more reliable territory. This is about people's lives, both the people who have just arrived here and the people who have been here for generations and have seen the world around them transformed. It is time to get serious. Fair and sensible immigration policy is hard to get right. We can't leave an issue this important to trouble-makers and nut-jobs.

If this book elbows fake news out the way, and replaces it with well-informed, well-argued conversation about one of the biggest issues of our time, then that is plenty to be pleased about, and reason enough to write these words. So let's get cracking, and start with the arrival of the *Windrush* and a man who casts a very long shadow over negative attitudes towards immigration.

# CHAPTER ONE
# THE DARK LEGACY OF ENOCH POWELL

Enoch Powell is one of the most notorious figures in twentieth-century British politics. He was also a very, very strange man.

Born in the summer of 1912, one of Powell's favourite games as a child was to jump onto the kitchen table and make speeches pretending to be the Prime Minister (the neighbours would be summoned to watch). Academically brilliant, he went off to Cambridge as an undergraduate, where he withdrew to what one biographer called 'an ascetic, almost monastic approach to life.' Powell's obsessive pursuit of intellectual success, which involved shunning the company of nearly all his peers, included teaching himself medieval Welsh. When he proposed to an early girlfriend, he managed to use language so steeped in classical learning that she didn't have a clue he had just asked to marry her.

By the time he became interested in politics, Powell sported a grand moustache styled on the nihilistic German philosopher Friedrich Nietzsche. In 1955 *The New Statesman* called Powell 'half-brilliant, half-mad.' Such was his passion for becoming an

MP that he referred to life on the backbenches in the House of Commons as 'coming home to mother.'[42]

And it was as a leading politician that Powell would emerge, by the end of the 60s, as the dominant anti-immigration voice in mainstream life. His 1968 Rivers of Blood speech, on what he imagined were the inevitable bloody consequences of immigration from Britain's ex-colonies, was one of the most memorable moments in a decade not short of political shocks.

We shall look at that notorious speech in more detail, but Powell's outburst did not come out of nowhere. It is worth thinking about the twenty years leading up to his speech, not least to find how his own views on immigration dramatically changed.

### 'Open to all'

In 1949 Powell was a deeply-ambitious thirty-something working for the Conservatives as a researcher, and was one of a small group of party thinkers who slaved over a document called *The right road for Britain*. With an election on the horizon, he and his colleagues were working long hours in the party's drab Victoria Street headquarters to try and guide future Conservative policy on everything from poor relief to rent controls. By the end of the year the document had been formally adopted by the party and published under Winston Churchill's name.

One section still jumps out. 'There must be freedom of movement among its members within the British Empire and Commonwealth,' the Conservatives wrote. 'New opportunities will present themselves not only in the countries overseas but in the Mother Country, and must be open to all citizens.'

Here was Powell, a man who would become famous for his hostility to immigration, enthusiastically pushing the moral case for keeping Britain's border open. He did not want any citizen of the empire or commonwealth denied the opportunities available to them in 'the mother country.' In 1949 that meant 800 million people, give or take. And while the Conservatives saw their free movement policy as part of the much larger political goal of shoring-up Britain's waning imperial role in the world, the idea of Powell lending his support to open borders still seems extraordinary.

## The *Windrush* years (see Figure 3)

It is even more striking given the events of the year before. It was in June 1948 that the HMS *Windrush* arrived at Tilbury Docks in Essex, probably the most iconic moment in modern immigration to the UK. Britain in the nineteenth century had not tried to control immigration, mainly because it was largely unthinkable that people would turn up un-announced on its borders, outside of existing trade routes. But the *Windrush* proved that people could and would do just that.

Four hundred and ninety-two passengers embarked (along with anything from one to eighteen stowaways, depending on which account you read),[43] having travelled the best part of five thousand miles from Britain's former colonies in the West Indies. As British citizens living in the commonwealth, they were responding to news of acute job shortages in Britain, which had been widely publicised on the islands.

They were here to help build a new economy. Hundreds more of their countrymen (and, to a lesser extent, countrywomen) would follow later in 1948 and 1949, then tens of thousands more in the years after that.

Figure 3. Source: Getty

Anti-immigration sentiments arose on the very same day the *Windrush* docked. Some Labour politicians wrote to the Prime Minister Clement Atlee, arguing that such immigration should be discouraged because newcomers would affect the 'harmony' of British society.[44] But Enoch Powell was seemingly among those who disagreed. Britain, he argued in that 1949 paper, must be open to immigration from its current and former colonies. Britain should welcome those who wanted to play their part in the nation's future.

This position didn't last, of course. By the mid-50s, Powell was publicly allowing that the British government *could* discriminate against the movement of some of its citizens based on their race, even if he wasn't yet committed to that sort of discrimination. By the end of the 60s this had metastasised into full-throated warnings that immigration would lead to social collapse.

But in the meantime, more and more people from the Caribbean were taking advantage of the chance to make their lives in Britain. The *Windrush* was only the beginning. Before the end of 1949 ships like the *Orbita* and the *Georgic* had followed in its wake. In each of the years between 1948 and 1952, around 1,000 to 2,000 West Indians entered Britain. Then numbers started to rise quickly: to 3,000 in 1953, then 10,000 in 1954, and then quadrupled to

42,000 the year after that. Roughly the same number arrived in 1956 and 1957, before dropping back below 30,000 towards the end of the decade.[45]

New arrivals on this scale, prominently discussed in the newspapers and by blustering politicians, would certainly have given a jolt to the existing population, even if it made a negligible difference to the lives of the overwhelming majority of Brits. Indeed, West Indian immigrants may have been forced to endure massive public attention in the 50s and 60s but they were vastly outnumbered by immigrants arriving from India and Pakistan (including the region which, after 1972, would become Bangladesh). According to the 1971 census, 479,000 people living in Britain had been born in South Asia by the turn of the century, more than double the number born in the Caribbean. And this wave of immigration pales into comparison next to movement from Ireland, which totalled more than a million.[46]

Nonetheless, it was the *Windrush* which proved fascinating at the time, and to commentators in later years. For one thing, not all the newcomers were strictly, well, newcomers. Half the men on the *Windrush* had actually served in the British army or RAF, fighting as part of the massive contingent of colonial soldiers, some of whom had been based on British soil during the war. The *Evening Standard* greeted the ship with the banner headline 'Welcome

Home', a slogan which probably referred to British commonwealth citizens returning to their 'mother land,' but which for some on board would have been truer than the headline-writer imagined.[47]

Whether they had never left the Caribbean before or were seasoned veterans of the British armed services, life was pretty tough for the new arrivals, 'a long hard slog' as Dominic Sandbrook describes it.[48] There were jobs available, as you would expect in an economy which so badly needed labour, but most work open to immigrants was menial and low-paid. Discrimination over housing started almost immediately (decent homes were much scarcer than employment after the bombing and destruction of the war).

Racial discrimination was rife, most overtly in the 'no blacks, no Irish, no dogs' signs that started to appear in windows of properties which were, supposedly, up for private rent. Few people frowned on this discrimination. 'It was perfectly common to see the phrases 'No Coloureds' or 'Whites Only' in newspaper advertisements or on cards posted on newsagents' noticeboards,' Sandbrook says.[49] When Caribbean citizens did find a private room to rent, they were so often over-charged that people started to refer to the extra cost as a 'colour tax.'

Public attitudes hardened over time. A 1961 poll found that barely one in five of the public wanted to keep the existing open border approach. Two-thirds wanted immigration restricted, and some wanted it to end completely.[50] The public cited housing and jobs as their main concerns, along with worries that Brits were being frozen out from public services by demand from immigrants, but there is little doubt that the response was also driven by open prejudice. The public was trying to get to grips with the idea that Britain's big cities were now host to thousands of black residents, a much newer and more controversial concept in the late 50s than it is now.

Meanwhile, the government did something which we will see governments do over and over again when confronted with tricky questions about immigration. They panicked. Ministers and officials chased around Whitehall, trying to find a way to stop British citizens in the West Indies from making a journey they were perfectly entitled to make.

The result was chaos. The government sent out bewildering mixed signals about immigration to a public who, unsurprisingly, didn't feel like they had much of a guide to what was going on around them.

It began with the legislation which paved the way for the arrival of so many West Indian immigrants. The 1948 British Nationality Act was, by any standard, an extraordinarily liberal bill. This is what extended British citizenship to anyone resident in Britain's empire and commonwealth, and with it the right to migrate to the mother country.*

This was the position the Conservatives were supporting in 1949 through *The right road for Britain* (not that this stopped Powell calling the British Nationality Act 'a deliberate act of self-humbug' years later, an impressive level of hypocrisy even for him).[51]

There was a big dose of imperial realpolitik at work here. The British Empire was slowly disintegrating, and the government wanted to maintain a hold over whatever remained, which meant ensuring free movement of trade and people in and out of those countries. This coincided with a desperate need for post-war labour in Britain – a Royal Commission in 1949 argued that 140,000 immigrants a year would fill the gaps as the economy started to recover and grow after the war, even if it didn't recommend this as a solution [52] – and news swiftly reached the Caribbean. The West Indians who flocked to Britain faced high unemployment at home and recognised the opportunity which had suddenly come their way. Jobs needed filling, including in the newly-established National Health Service, and the islands boasted plenty of people keen to fill them.

Except that what had been clear in the Caribbean apparently wasn't clear to the British govern-

---

* Some historians argue that these rights meant commonwealth citizens heading to Britain should no more be considered 'immigrants' than someone leaving Yorkshire for London. This is a compelling argument, although for consistency across the book we will stick with the term.

ment. Ministers and officials had assumed, in a way which was both complacently vague and implicitly racist, that if anyone came to Britain it would be residents of what were sometimes called the 'white dominions' of Canada, New Zealand, South Africa or Australia. They had never imagined that black citizens would come, even while they passed legislation which explicitly made this possible.

As the light dawned, and in the earliest signs of panic, civil servants were dispatched to the islands to try and discourage people from setting out. There was even an eleventh-hour discussion about diverting the *Windrush* to Kenya and encouraging those on board to become nut farmers there instead. Unsurprisingly, this idea was swiftly ditched.

It was a shambles. The government, having passed legislation which opened up Britain to immigration from the commonwealth, duly heard that these British citizens were on their way and tried to stop them coming. When these attempts failed, they were left muddling along trying to accommodate and integrate newcomers who had arrived to do jobs that the British economy desperately needed.

The newcomers were fellow citizens, 'men and brothers with the people of this country,' the Labour Home Secretary told the House of Commons. This was an admirable attempt to generate support and solidarity, but when Winston Churchill's Conservatives were returned to power in 1951 this was in thinner supply.

Churchill took one look at public opinion and set about finding ways to stem the flow of immigrants. As David Olusoga puts it:

> In the early 1950s, Churchill asked government officials in various departments to devise mechanisms by which West Indians might be kept out of the country, contrary to the rights of entry and residency they enjoyed under the 1948 Nationality Act. The challenge was to draft legislation that specifically targeted non-white immigrants while not appearing to be motivated by racial considerations.[53]

Churchill was unanimously backed in this by senior colleagues in government, but he hit an insurmountable problem. He needed evidence that the migration of lots of black Caribbean citizens into Britain had caused problems – but that evidence didn't exist. As another historian, Winston James, says:

> Building a 'strong case' [to block immigration from the Caribbean] involved the gathering and analysing of data to show that black settlers constituted a 'problem' which called for targeted immigration controls. Successive working parties could never

find enough negative information to make a case sufficiently persuasive to win parliamentary and public approval.[54]

Churchill repeatedly tried to find an excuse for blocking black immigration over the years, and he failed each time. Commonwealth citizens in Britain simply weren't causing any problems for the country. There was objectively no need whatsoever to bar them from coming.

It is worth bearing in mind that under 2,000 West Indians arrived in Britain in the year Churchill started his fruitless hunt for reasons to block their passage. As so often, panic about immigration ran well ahead of *actual* immigration.

But panic was still being stoked, and a familiar figure was about to return to the fray.

## Powell the politician

Enoch Powell was by now a Conservative MP in Wolverhampton and the Minister for Health under Prime Minister Harold MacMillan. The location of Powell's constituency gives some indication of why he started thinking about immigration, but only some. He made a big fuss about seeing the impact of immigration first-hand on his own patch, and it is estimated that Wolverhampton was home to around

1,000 West Indian immigrants by the late 50s. It was certainly a big enough change to provoke conversations among local politicians but paled in comparison to the number of people settling in London and Birmingham.[55]

Nonetheless, Powell decided in 1961 that the situation was serious enough that he should elbow his way into the committee which advised on immigration policy, and in this way got to have his say in designing the Commonwealth Immigrants Act. That Act went through parliament the following year, but Powell's evolution into an anti-immigrant politician was now well underway. His idealism about empire and the commonwealth had only ever worked in one direction, it turned out. The abstract idea of British values expanding across the globe appealed to him, but when the commonwealth started to arrive on his doorstep he saw nothing but the potential for trouble. It is intriguing to imagine how different things could have been if Powell had put his brilliant mind to the very real challenge of making immigration and integration work for his constituents, helping residents and newcomers build a shared sense of the future together, amid the growth of new cultural identities and worries about fair access to jobs and housing. It would have been a very different legacy – but the idea appears never to have occurred to him.

To Powell's frustration, the 1962 Act didn't freeze commonwealth citizens out of immigration rights completely, but it still went a pretty long way to roll back the liberal intent of the legislation from the 40s. Under the new law, any commonwealth citizen who didn't have a direct connection to Britain or a government voucher offering employment (the number of which were tightly controlled) wasn't allowed to cross the border.

Except, as Whitehall should have predicted, commonwealth citizens got wind of these new restrictions and rushed to fulfil their travel plans before the regulations took effect. As a result, more immigrants came to Britain in the eighteen months before the Commonwealth Immigrants Act became law than in the entire preceding five years, including 66,000 people from the Caribbean. Not for the first time, the public would have seen immigration grow at the same time that ministers, speaking in parliament and in the newspapers, were promising to bring it down.

It is in precisely these sorts of moments that trust in politicians is lost – and that demagogues can strike. As he campaigned during the 1964 general election, Powell told voters that it was time to restrict commonwealth immigration, fully aware that it *had* been restricted two years before, thanks to his own efforts on the 1961 committee. If this helped raise tensions unnecessarily, he went even further when he pointedly refused to condemn stickers reading 'If you want a n****r neighbour, vote Labour,' which were plastered over the neighbouring constituency.

And so it went on. Powell wanted to block Kenyan Asians from coming to Britain, even though their right to travel here was guaranteed under the very 1962 Commonwealth Immigrants Act he had helped shape. He railed against the introduction of laws to stop landlords discriminating against immigrants, which were eventually passed in 1965, because he believed governments should leave people to handle their own private affairs (not an unreasonable political philosophy, but most people would still have drawn a line at those 'no blacks' signs). In 1967 he wrote in *The Telegraph* that the government, by letting immigrants transform the communities they moved into, was betraying voters.[56]

By the late 60s, Powell's argument for cutting commonwealth immigration was that existing immigrants had not integrated, and that any further arrivals would make this problem worse. Certainly, integration was proving extremely tricky on all sides. As the years had rolled on, white gangs who had generally just fought one another suddenly had a common target. Black immigrants were in the firing line, some of whom had shown they were up for a fight, too. In the most dramatic scenes, hundreds of white residents in poor areas like St Ann's in Bristol and London's Notting Hill went on the rampage in 1958, looking for black immigrants to beat up.[57] Dozens of people were injured. Even though it was low-level discrimination which probably had the biggest impact on life for Britain's immigrants, reports of teenagers with flick knives going 'n****r bashing' heightened the national sense that greater immigration was bringing social tensions, even when immigrants were the victims.

A guiding hand from some senior politicians would have been helpful, and by 1965 Labour had introduced the first Race Relations Act – an extremely welcome step to try and level the playing field for immigrants in work and housing, but not one backed by Powell. Worse still, the language he used even before the Rivers of Blood speech was designed to inflame tensions, and could only make integration harder. In that *Telegraph* article, Powell drew on chest-beating, military metaphors for readers who would have remembered the terror of the Second World War all too well. 'Acts of an enemy, bombs from the sky' were one thing, Powell wrote, but through immigration Britain now faced a comparable threat, an 'invasion,' 'bulldozers,' and 'shattered lives' left in its wake.

These are not the words of a man seeking a solution to a problem, but one trying to foment hostility, even as occasional race riots sparked-up. And his most famous act of provocation was just around the corner.

## Rivers of blood

In April 1968, Powell rose to make the speech which ended his political career but made him a household name to this day. One of the most controversial events in modern political history was about to take place, in the unlikely surroundings of the annual general meeting of the West Midlands Area Conservative Political Centre in Birmingham.

The speech was three thousand words long. It would have taken Powell about twenty minutes to read it. Not everything he said was new – he had been honing his anti-immigration rhetoric for years – but it was the first time so many of his views were concentrated in a single speech.[58]

His opposition to any legislation which would protect immigrants from exploitation was there, as was his inflammatory language. Equal rights laws would 'risk throwing a match on to gunpowder'; the failure to restrict immigration further 'is like watching a nation busily engaged in heaping up its own funeral pyre'; he quoted a constituent who told him 'In this country in fifteen or twenty years' time, the black man will have the whip hand over the white man.'

Having shown no interest in helping Brits and immigrants integrate, Powell now alleged that 'a growing majority' of new arrivals from the commonwealth had no interest in integration anyway:

> There are among the Commonwealth immigrants who have come to live here in the last fifteen years or so, many thousands whose wish and purpose is to be integrated and whose every thought and endeavour is bent in that direction. But to imagine that such a thing enters the heads of a great and growing majority of immigrants and their descendants is a ludicrous misconception, and a dangerous one.

In the most famous passage of the speech, Powell argued that if immigrants continued to come to Britain and enjoy even basic legal protections, this would mean:

> that the immigrant communities can organise to consolidate their members, to agitate and campaign against their fellow citizens, and to overawe and dominate the rest with the legal weapons which the ignorant and the ill-informed have provided. As I look ahead, I am filled with foreboding; like the Ro-

man, I seem to see 'the River Tiber foaming with much blood.'

Having foreseen blood and carnage, Powell offered the only remedy he could think of: he called for an almost complete halt to immigration and argued that people who had been making their lives in Britain for two decades should be encouraged to pack their things and leave.

Even sympathetic commentators recognised that the speech 'adopted an increasingly apocalyptic tone.'[59] This wasn't a plan for dealing with immigration but a rallying-cry of intolerance and anger. If you were an immigrant, Powell had just one suggestion for you: go home.

It was all too much for Powell's boss, Tory leader Ted Heath. Heath sacked Powell from his frontbench the next morning, citing both Powell's disloyalty in opposing the official government line on immigration and the tone of the speech.

## The fall

There is something genuinely sad about the way Powell's career veered downhill from here.

No doubt buoyed by the idea that he and he alone was willing to say out loud what others dared not admit – and certainly he enjoyed substantial support from voters who praised him for speaking 'common sense' – he burnished subsequent speeches with increasingly outlandish conspiracy theories and outright lies. He repeated the claim that one school in his constituency had a class where there was only one white child (this wasn't true), and that black immigrant gangs had posted excrement through the door of a local woman (this wasn't true either – in fact, it was an apocryphal tale much favoured by anti-immigration campaigners in every region of the country, which Powell had now given a political platform).[60]

In the run up to the 1970 general election he took another leap, and now wanted to separate families by barring wives and children from joining loved-ones in Britain (a position nearly all mainstream politicians, Powell previously included, had dismissed as inhumane).[61]

Powell may have been a classical scholar but some of his interventions were now more reminiscent of a pub bore. In one speech he imagined that, as MP for the increasingly diverse Wolverhampton, he might be seen as 'a Member of Parliament for Central Africa.'[62] His local paper, which had stuck with him through years of controversy, started begging Powell to stop using such cruel language about immigration, but to no avail.

By the 70s, Powell was alleging that the Home Office was collaborating with the Foreign Office to suppress the 'true' number of babies being born to immigrant families. Not content with this, in 1984 his favourite theory held that an ally of Margaret Thatcher had been killed not by Irish Republicans but by a coalition of the Foreign Office, British secret services and the CIA. Asked to produce evidence to support his ludicrous claims Powell could, of course, produce nothing.[63]

## The damage done

Some commentators took the centenary of Powell's birth in 2012 as an opportunity to try and revive his public reputation and re-present him as a man willing to tell unpalatable truths about immigration to which the British establishment remained deaf. But he wasn't a champion of the people, he was a disaster.

His speeches hurt commonwealth immigrants, who were attacked and whose homes were torched in the febrile atmosphere he had helped encourage. And he hurt the communities into which immigrants moved, too, because – for all the predictions of disaster Powell enjoyed delivering – he offered absolutely nothing that would help those communities integrate, let alone grow and thrive. Powell was

fond of talking about the duties of a great statesman
(a role he had imagined himself in ever since those
days as a toddler delivering speeches from the kitch-
en table), but he took no steps to translate this into
the sort of difficult but vital work on the ground
which could have helped his constituents build their
lives together.

Ultimately, and maybe most depressingly of all,
Powell had no idea of the damage he had caused.
When the black British MP Paul Boateng spoke
publicly in 1995 about the abuse he had suffered as
a child in the backlash caused by Powell's speech,
Powell, now in his eighties, simply batted his concerns away. When other ethnic minority families
told him the same thing in later years Powell was,
says one biographer, 'genuinely surprised.'[64]

It is an extraordinary admission: all this talk of
powder kegs and blood running on British streets,
of telling settled immigrants to move back to countries they had left decades before, the quotes about
black immigrants having the 'whip hand' over white
people – yet Powell airily assumed this would have
no effect on the lives of people who had moved to
Britain to help build its future.

He never did say sorry. Given the chance years
later to build bridges with colleagues he had upset,
'Powell was unrepentant.'[65]

## The state of things to come

There is one more striking thing about Powell. When we hear about the hostile environment confronting migrants today there is a decent chance we will hear echoes of his rhetoric.

He was, for example, the first mainstream politician of this modern age to smear immigrants with unfounded accusations about draining the health service. Back in 1961, Powell won his place advising the Conservatives on immigration policy by arguing that he had seen first-hand the negative impact of immigration in his Wolverhampton constituency. His concern about the demand immigrants placed on local doctors and hospitals – with evidence seemingly drawn from a single report by a single local council – is especially hypocritical. As Health Minister, Powell also set the targets for attracting the immigrants needed to keep the NHS running. Every time we hear a spurious attack on health tourism, we should remember that Powell got there first.

He also fell out with Margaret Thatcher because she had refused, when Education Secretary, to collect data on immigrant children in schools. Move forward to 2010 (and chapter four of this book), and we can see Theresa May's anti-immigrant agenda playing out as schools and hospitals are forced to gather and share more information on the immigration background of pupils and patients.

NHS stories confected for political gain? The angriest voice demanding that the state intrude on the lives of immigrant kids? The anti-immigrant pioneer who knew emigration could ruin the economy but told people to leave the country anyway? Hostile ideas each and every one, and Powell was the intellectual father of them all.

He was a strange man, for sure, but he was a dangerous one too.

# CHAPTER TWO
# SHUT THAT DOOR

One thing was clear as the 60s turned into the 70s. Britain, in particular London and the big cities, *had* changed. There were many more people with dark skin, there was new food and music and culture on the streets, there were more ways to be British. It all stirred strong opinions, even if for the majority of people life remained almost entirely untouched by immigration.

The Rivers of Blood speech no doubt influenced how immigration was viewed, but people didn't need to subscribe to Enoch Powell's grim worldview to worry about the changes taking place. Brits were pretty sceptical. In one 1968 Gallup poll, 61% judged that commonwealth immigration had harmed the country; only 16% thought Britain had benefitted.[66] The post-war immigration boom was twenty years old, and people were wary of its effect.

This ushered in a consensus at the top of politics which would last the best part of thirty years: that immigration should be greatly limited or even shut down completely. A newfound confidence about the benefits of immigration re-emerged with a vengeance as the millennium loomed – but until then, there were a tough few decades ahead for Britain's new immigrants and their British-born children.

## Unwelcome

For too many people at this time, Britain was downright scary.

'I imbibed enough of the background racial tensions of the late 1970s and 1980s to feel profoundly unwelcome in Britain,' writes the Nigerian-born historian David Olusoga of his childhood growing up in north-east England. 'The political aether had been poisoned by the politics of hate.'

'Almost every black or mixed-race person of my generation has a story of racial violence to tell,' he adds later. 'These stories range from humiliation to hospitalization.'[67]

And for some even death. 'Daily life for the Bengali and Pakistani families in the area became torrid,' says Robert Winder of the capital in the 70s, before reeling-off a frightening list of some casualties from what he calls the decade's 'bitter and one-sided social war':

> Ishaque Ali was beaten up in Hackney; Kayimarz Anblesaria was kicked to death at Bromley-by-Bow underground station; Akhtar Ali Baig was stabbed

in East Ham. And it wasn't confined to London: Satnam Singh Gill was knifed in Coventry; Samira Kassam, who had three small sons and was pregnant with another, was killed when raiders set fire to her house in Ilford; Ahmed Iqbal, a thirteen-year-old Bangladeshi boy, was stabbed on his way to school.[68]

One child of the 70s, the son of an Irish mum and a West Indian dad, reflected on growing up in south London: 'If 'paki-bashing' had been an Olympic sport, my part of town would have won a gold medal.' [69]

The stories are plentiful, frightening, and bloody. There were calls for decency from some quarters – immigrants 'are citizens of this country, here to build a new life for themselves and their families,' said an editorial in *The Mirror* in the summer of 1969, 'it is as fellow citizens and fellow human beings that they are entitled to be accepted'[70] – but it was the skinhead thugs of the National Front who were ascendant on the streets, leaving people terrified in their wake. 'One down, a million to go,' boasted National Front leader John Kingsley Read after the racist murder of Gurdip Singh Chaggar in Southall in 1976.[71]

Briefly, the National Front also threatened to make an impact via the ballot box. Two of its candidates secured more than 10% in parliamentary by-elections during the 70s, but this was the high watermark. Hundreds more wannabe National Front MPs barely scraped to 1% or 2%. With the benefit of hindsight this is a great relief, but would have meant little to those at the time being chased, beaten and terrorised in British towns.[72]

Some of these tensions at the start of the 70s emerged from the naked racism embodied by the National Front, some from the hangover left by Rivers of Blood, some from an ailing economy (of which more below), some from a popular fear of change. These overlapped and intersected, of course. But the government also played its own, unhelpful role. One message was being clearly projected to the country: one of hostility to immigrants. Britain was better off without them.

## Raising the drawbridge

Britain's post-war immigration boom was coming to an end. Commonwealth immigration during the 70s and 80s settled down to about 50,000 people each year, and maybe as importantly it took on more predictable patterns. The days of sudden growth and steep declines in immigration numbers were over, for now.

'The decades of the 1950s, 1960s and 1990s stand out as those in which the strongest growth in the

UK's foreign-born population occurred,' as the data crunchers at the Office for National Statistics put it years later. Compared with those decades, 'the rate of growth of the foreign-born population over the 1970s and 1980s was much lower.'

The ONS was also clear that this slowing had not happened by chance: 'Part of the explanation is the introduction of legislation that restricted immigration channels which had previously been open to residents of the former British colonies of South Asia and the Caribbean.'[73]

They were probably thinking about Labour's 1968 Commonwealth Immigrants Act, which (even before Rivers of Blood) successfully blocked thousands of Asians in Kenya from their plans to head to Britain. But it was the Conservative's 1971 Immigration Act which really applied the kind of swingeing restrictions politicians had been threatening for decades. It stripped British citizens in the commonwealth of the right to come and live in Britain, and made their British passports meaningless overnight. (This also paved the way for the mistreatment of *Windrush* families more than forty years later, as we shall see in Chapter Four).

Unless someone had a permit for a specific job in a specific place, the country had been closed-off to new workers from overseas. Even if immigrants *were* working here, they were now obliged to report to the police every twelve months, establishing a pernicious link between immigration and crime which would prove irresistible to generations of politicians to come.

The 1971 Act was also – and there is no gentle way to put this – racist.

Some commonwealth citizens *would* be able to travel to Britain without too much bother, thanks to an exemption designed exclusively to help white immigrants. The Act protected something called the 'partial right of abode', through which people could still come and go if one of their parents or grandparents had been born in Britain. In practice, this meant that the door was still open to children born to white families across the old empire but had been slammed shut on children born to black families.

In the vocabulary of the time, it introduced a 'colour bar' into British legislation, the very thing that politicians had spent years trying to avoid. Winston Churchill may have *wanted* to discriminate against black immigrants back in the 50s, but he couldn't find even the flimsy justification he felt he needed. By the early 70s, politicians had stopped even bothering to look for justification. The Home Secretary Reginald Maudling made a predictably bad fist of pretending that colour had nothing to do with it ('of course they are more likely to be white, because we have on the whole more whites than coloured in this country,' he told the press, an impressively circular argument for why white immigrants might benefit from legislation created precisely to help them), but no one was fooled.[74]

The sound heard around the world was that of a drawbridge being raised.

## Economic woes

Powell had barely gone quiet, the government was embedding racism through legislation, and the National Front was on the front foot. As if this wasn't enough bad news for immigrants and their families there was one more piece of the jigsaw still to come: the economy.

The association between the 70s and economic chaos is justified. It was a volatile decade, and immigrants were on the frontline as families across Britain struggled to get by. In 1975 inflation was a whopping 27%. Between 1970 and 1980 the cost of household food (bread, milk, eggs, a decent cut of meat) rose four-fold. And while it was also a period when wage growth was negotiated upward at similar levels (sometimes with a quiet word between industry and the government, sometimes off the back of strikes and protests), the main effect was chronic instability. It was 'difficult for people to keep a basic idea of what a unit of currency was actually worth,' writes the historian Andy McSmith.[75]

Unemployment was also a serious problem. By the 80s it topped 3 million, peaking at an absolutely wretched 12% of the working-age population, but great swathes of workers were affected well before that. Official stats show that 1.1 million British people were out of work by the end of the 70s, an unthinkable number after such a long period where the economy needed labour.[76]

This combination – of spiralling inflation, uncertainty and high unemployment – hit people across British society. It was a tragedy for families all over the country. And it especially hit people in menial jobs and on low wages, the very area of the economy in which many immigrants from preceding years now found themselves.

As McSmith puts it, 'generally, to be black meant to be consigned to a low-paid job or no job at all, to live in substandard housing in an inner-city ghetto and to have your children go to one of the worst state schools. In a recession, the ethnic minorities were hit first.'[77]

Dominic Sandbrook, looking at the experience of Asian as well as Caribbean immigrants, says:

[S]ince the mills and factories that would once have given newcomers a foothold on the ladder were closing down, they often found themselves condemned to low-paid manual jobs in dreary, dilapidated, depressed towns that the rest of Britain had forgotten. By 1975, government figures showed that unemployment among immigrants was twice the national average, while young black school-leavers were four times less likely than their white counterparts to find jobs.[78]

The failing economy wasn't the only thing at play here, of course: racist discrimination wasn't rare among employers, even after race relations acts had come into force, and certainly employees who got racist abuse from colleagues and bosses (sometimes dressed up as banter or off-colour jokes) were largely expected to put up with it or leave. But the economic situation made this all the more pronounced, as workers from all backgrounds fought to protect themselves from lay-offs and the uncertain value of their pay packets.

Society had become harder and more closed. The tricky work of integration – of immigrants and Brits finding a way to live together with the fewest possible bumps in the road – became much more difficult. There is certainly an argument that forcing down immigration numbers could aid integration by slowing the pace of social change and giving everyone a more stable environment in which to think about Britain's new-look communities. The same case is made today. But the government's decision publicly to back the desirability of white immigrants over the undesirability of black immigrants undid any sense that this was a time of opportunity and coming together.

This was what Britain looked like as the 70s got into full swing. It wasn't an encouraging setting for good news about immigration, and two episodes illustrate how hostile the government remained during the decade. The first shows how much more impressive normal Brits were than local and national government when it came to looking after new immigrants. The second shows how easily and readily the state assumed the power to demean and humiliate immigrants in the name of keeping low numbers still lower.

## Big trouble in Uganda

At the start of 1971, almost no one in Britain would have heard of Idi Amin. But Amin's behaviour thousands of miles away in Uganda was about to create a refugee crisis for tens of thousands of Ugandans and a political crisis for the British establishment.

Major General Idi Amin took power in Kampala through a coup in January. This was initially greeted with some cheer in Whitehall. Not only had Amin removed an unpopular, corrupt government, but British officials couldn't have crafted a better imperial subject if they had tried. Eight years on from Ugandan independence, Amin boasted the exemplary credentials of a military man brought up under the British Empire: a keen boxer, a member of the colonial regiment of the King's African Rifles, a promising rugby player (fittingly for a man of his bulk, he was a second row forward). 'We always thought that Amin was a decent chap,' one civil servant wrote at the time.[79]

He was nothing of the sort. Erratic and brutal, Amin announced plans in 1972 to expel several tens of thousands of Ugandan Asians from his country. A sizeable number of Asian migrants, mainly from India, had settled across west Africa in previous generations, often taking up jobs in senior professions in the public sector, and they now stood accused of living a life of comfort at the expense of 'real' Ugandans.

It was ugly populism from a cruel ruler and it threw the lives of Ugandan Asians into immediate crisis. There was a looming deadline for them to leave or face likely violence, but to where? For some, the answer was obvious. Around sixty thousand Ugandan Asians held British passports, so surely Britain could take them in?

At first the Conservative government dithered. The cabinet was torn between a humanitarian impulse to look after people who clearly had an urgent need for sanctuary and a public still unhappy about levels of immigration even after the new legislation. It was Reginald Maudling – the Home Secretary, remember, who had introduced a legal colour bar into the immigration rules – who argued it would be indecent (and by implication un-British) for the country to turn its back during the Ugandan Asians' hour of need.[80]

Having tried and failed to redirect people from Uganda to other commonwealth islands, the government bowed to pressure to take in refugees. Ministers established the Uganda Resettlement Board to work out how many and to try and co-ordinate their reception, including where this latest tranche of immigrants might end up living. The board did a good job in a short time, but it also scored an impressive own goal when it produced a map of Britain covered in red dots, intended to indicate areas of the country that refugees should avoid because immigration was already high. All this did was guide the eye towards bits of Britain where Ugandan Asians might be guaranteed a stronger welcome. Accordingly, many Ugandans decided to head that way.

One city decorated with a red dot was Leicester. Leicester Council had looked at the large number of Asian immigrants already settled in the city and decided that it didn't want any more. In fact, councillors were so keen to close the door that the local authority took the extraordinary step of paying for an advert to appear in the *Uganda Argus*, one of the national newspapers in Kampala.

It was a move even more foolish than the board's scattering of red dots. In September 1972, Ugandans woke up to an ad in their own press, placed there by councillors half the world away, urging in block capitals: 'IN YOUR OWN INTERESTS AND THOSE OF YOUR FAMILY YOU SHOULD ACCEPT THE ADVICE OF THE UGANDA RE-SETTLEMENT BOARD AND NOT COME TO LEICESTER.'[81]

It didn't put people off the city so much as act as an advert for Leicester, and where the council faltered in its humanitarian duty, normal citizens did not. By the end of 1972, 5,000 Leicester residents had offered up space in their own homes to refugees, in a scheme organised largely but not exclusively by the city's Asian population. They raised £10,000 (something more like £140,000 in today's money) and took possession of more than two hundred and fifty homes to offer refugees somewhere to live. Crucially, these were homes otherwise earmarked for demolition, which meant no newcomer would dislodge Brits waiting on the list for social housing. This was a far smarter bit of local politics than anything the council managed. Housing was a flashpoint in immigration debates, then as now, and the idea that refugees could jump the queue for scarce homes would have started the whole project on a much more controversial footing. Leicester's campaigners were canny enough to anticipate the danger and work around it.[82] The British public may have been sceptical about immigration, but they were also sensible of the need to help people in need and of the the conditions required to get this right.

There was opposition, of course, but in this case it was local communities who understood the importance of integration. The solution was imperfect and hastily cobbled together, but when refugees did arrive in Leicester they found a city which had prepared for their presence and where locals were relatively well-informed about the new arrivals and determined to make it work. It is surely no coincidence that of all the communities which have found a home in modern Britain, it is the Ugandan Asians who integrated and thrived economically with particular speed. These days Leicester is rather proud of how everything turned out.

By the end of 1973 around 25,000 Ugandan Asian refugees had made new lives in Britain (much less than 50,000 or even 100,000, numbers bandied around by some in the media). Thousands more found safety in Canada or Australia. And if Leicester's Ugandan Asians muddled through better than most, it was because of the semi-organised commitment of local Brits, who had shown more generosity and greater nous than the politicians around them.

## Embarrassed and ashamed

If the people of Leicester can tell a story about citizens coming together to make immigration work more smoothly, the 70s also saw one of the most shameful episodes in modern immigration history. It affected relatively few people and originated from an obscure inconsistency in immigration rules, but there is no better example of how cruelly intrusive the authorities could become.

Immigration to Britain had changed. In the years immediately after the war, it had been dominated by men, mainly young workers in search of jobs. But as those men started to settle in their new home, so their families wanted to join them. By 1971, three-quarters of all immigrants were women and children, the majority either reuniting with their loved-ones or joining husbands for marriages arranged across the continents.

For governments looking to force migration numbers down, this put, in particular, young women from Pakistan and India in the firing-line. A quirk in the rules meant that a woman from overseas visiting her British husband needed to wait a year for a visa to enter the country. However, a woman visiting her fiancé could travel whenever she wished, so long as the happy day was less than three months away.

British authorities swiftly realised that newly-married couples probably wouldn't be thrilled at being separated for a year. Officials got it into their heads that women might pretend to be a fiancée rather than a wife so that they could sneak into the country a little more quickly.

The solution reached at the Home Office was a physical exam, conducted by a doctor at the airport, to decide whether or not the traveller was a virgin. Accounts from the time suggest that wives and fiancées alike were pulled aside for exams when they arrived at Heathrow. It is now thought that around eighty women were examined, although this is only the number for Heathrow.[83] The same procedure was also conducted at visa centres in foreign capitals, which means British authorities almost certainly conducted far more exams than we know about. These numbers may be just 'the tip of the iceberg,' academics have warned.[84]

One woman from Pakistan who touched down in Heathrow in 1976 recalled her introduction to Britain: 'I went through immigration and then I was sent aside for a medical. They took me to a room. They asked me to undress and made me lie down, and then they did it.'

'I was young, I went along with it,' she added, remembering the 'deep embarrassment' of it all. 'All I wanted was to get outside and join my husband. We were newlyweds and I couldn't wait to see him.'

'They were only asking the women who were travelling on their own to go to one side,' another Pakistani woman said. 'It was embarrassing and it also felt a little shameful.'[85]

The Home Office has long resisted attempts to uncover the whole story. Indeed, it even successfully hid these details for many years. But virginity testing was part of immigration control on British soil from 1975 and possibly earlier. It was apparently stopped in 1979 – although this was because of a diplomatic row it created in India rather than because of any outcry about violating women's bodies.

The official welcome to Britain involved embarrassment, suspicion and, out of nowhere, a clinical procedure. Of all the indecencies suffered by people arriving in Britain, this is the moment where it seems most extraordinary that newcomers here accepted how they had been treated, kept faith in their new country, and made a life for themselves and for their families.

This was the mood music for the seventies: violence on the streets, hostile legislation, immigrants pitched into even greater competition over scarce jobs, and a response among officials which veered from panic over Uganda to abuse against young women as they stepped onto British soil. It is a credit to immigrants and residents alike that so many found a way, amid the chaos, to carry on together with relatively little fuss.

## Thatcher and an 'end to immigration'

All this was before the arrival of the political figure who would dominate the next decade and more.

Margaret Thatcher emerged, as we saw in chapter one, with some credit from the Enoch Powell saga, although it was hardly difficult for a politician to position themselves to the left of Powell on immigration. Her own career began to take off just as Powell's entered terminal decline, and by the time she became Conservative Prime Minister in 1979 – reaching the pinnacle of British politics which Powell so craved – she had already established her own, grim position on immigration. Thatcher's agenda was marked from the beginning by talking up the threats posed by immigration while making promises which her government couldn't possibly meet. It was exactly the combination Britain had seen in the 50s and 60s, and it was just as likely to breed problems.

In January 1978 Thatcher, then leader of the opposition, sat down for an interview on ITV's *World
in Action*.[86] *World in Action* was one of the country's
flagship current affairs programmes, with viewing
figures which sometimes reached a staggering 23
million. Decades before Twitter or Facebook, if political figures wanted to get their messages out to the
public then this was one of the main ways to achieve
it.

The broadcast would become famous for the
language Thatcher used to describe immigration;
but it deserves attention, too, for the specific, hard-
line promise she made to voters.

Thatcher, decked-out in a navy blue suit and
sitting forward on a high-backed, gold-upholstered
chair, which looked suspiciously like a throne, was
asked about immigration. 'Some people have felt
swamped by immigrants,' she replied. 'They've
seen the whole character of their neighbourhoods
changed.' She continued: 'We do have to hold out
the prospect of an end to immigration except of
course for compassionate cases.' (These 'compassionate' circumstances went undefined; although
she presumably meant letting husbands and wives
join their spouses here.)

Thatcher had more to say – immigrants bringing
their own faiths and cultures to Britain were compared with the 'British character [which] has done

so much for democracy, for law,' a very short version of world history which would have surprised experts on centuries of international scholarship – but it is the language of 'swamped' and the promise of 'an end to immigration' which most merit a closer look.

The word 'swamped' was not chosen by chance. Thatcher wanted to take us back to the rhetoric ushered in by Powell and his fellow travellers, and to a time when politicians were trying to force hostile language into the political mainstream. Here was the leader of the opposition, giving it a platform once again.

But the language also set the stage for Thatcher's promise on immigration, which she was careful to make not once but twice. No more immigrants would enter Britain on her watch, or as she put it 'either you go on taking in forty or fifty thousand [immigrants] a year, which is far too many, or you say we must hold out the prospect of a clear end to immigration, and this is the view we have taken.'

Thatcher was making a more radical proposal than some commentators have recognised. The language is precise. She isn't just talking about commonwealth immigrants but *all* immigration. She wanted to 'hold out the prospect' of immigration ending completely, to dangle that possibility in front of the British public as they decided how to vote in 1979. Forty or fifty thousand immigrants each year was forty or fifty thousand too many, she was saying. All this needed to end.

And did immigration end? No, of course not. What Thatcher achieved was to bring common-wealth immigration down to slightly lower and more predictable levels, at around 50,000 a year (precisely the rate that she had declared to be 'far too many'). Voters were told to fear immigration and offered the idea that it could end completely – but immigration continued nonetheless. In fact, immigration by mainly white citizens from countries like Australia, South Africa and the United States went *up*. This clearly worried Thatcher little if at all. McSmith concludes that it was all 'entirely a matter about race,'[87] and it is hard to disagree.

There is one postscript to all this. As Thatcher would have known, more people were leaving Britain than arriving in the last years of the 70s. Net migration had been negative every year between 1975 and 1978, and there wouldn't be positive immigration of any substance until 1983. Brits were heading for Australia, Canada, New Zealand and South Africa in record numbers.[88] To borrow Thatcher's language, immigration wasn't 'swamping' the country, it was part of a receding tide. But that isn't what she told voters.

## Posturing

If Thatcher's first act was to pledge zero immigration, her second, once in government, was to force through a law which achieved little, apart from symbolising her promised tough line on immigrants.

By 1981, Willie Whitelaw, the Home Secretary and a key Thatcher ally – 'every prime minister needs a Willie,' she once said – was ushering in new legislation to remove, in his words, any 'lingering notion that Britain is somehow a haven for all those whose countries we used to rule.'[89]

In truth, that notion hadn't lingered anywhere for years. Previous legislation had killed the idea stone dead, and Whitelaw didn't do much to hide the fact that this was political posturing more than it was essential policy-making. Having agreed that spouses could still join their families in Britain (the 'compassionate' cases to which Thatcher referred) there was precious little the government could do to tighten immigration further. The 1981 Immigration Act now separated British nationality into three tiers – full citizenship, dependent territories citizenship and British overseas citizenship – and full rights were extended only to full citizens. When this came into force in 1983, the drawbridge had been cranked that bit higher for all but a few immigrants moving into key professions.

Whitelaw was responding not to facts on the ground but to pure perception, the 'lingering notion' that borders were as open in the 80s as they had been in the 40s. And why did this absurd notion linger on? Because Thatcher had gone on primetime television to talk about it. She had justified further anti-immigration laws and stoked tensions a little more.

## All change

This is how things continued, as the Conservatives ruled on and on into the next decade. Exhausted after years in office, the Tories collapsed and Tony Blair and New Labour stormed to power in 1997. They did so with a big enough majority to start transforming Britain extremely quickly. This was nowhere truer than in immigration.

The new regime rolled-back years of restrictions introduced by past Conservative and Labour governments alike. 'Britain's economic immigration policy went from a highly restrictive approach to one of the most expansive in Europe,' notes researcher Erica Consterdine.[90] Many of the barriers erected to hold immigration at bay were swiftly dismantled. Immigration shot up accordingly after 1997, in a way unseen for more than a generation.

Work permits were given out much more freely. The number of foreign students coming to Britain doubled, not least because New Labour wanted a slice of a foreign student market worth billions. It got easier for immigrants to bring their families to join them. Around 2.5 million foreign-born workers were added to the British population in New Labour's tenure. And as immigration boomed, so it boosted the economy and bolstered institutions that Brits love most. An NHS recruitment drive in 2000 meant 9,500 more doctors and 20,000 more nurses from overseas.[91]

In later years there was a distracting spat about exactly why Labour did what it did. The vast majority of Labour types argued that loosening immigration controls was just sensible economic policy suited to a global order on the cusp of a new millennium, even if it set up political problems they hadn't anticipated. Not quite, said one party aide, Andrew Neather. Opening up Britain to the world, Neather wrote, 'was intended – even if this wasn't its main purpose – to rub the Right's nose in diversity, and render their arguments out of date.'[92] Other Labour insiders dismiss his theories as nonsense.

Whatever the motives, the drawbridge had been lowered again. People were soon making their homes and their livelihoods in Britain in their hundreds of thousands, even before citizens from the new A10

EU states were offered the chance to join them after 2004. The economy was booming and many immigrants deserved their reputation for their work ethic. The British public, sceptical as ever, watched on with growing unease, but they also gave credit where it was due, albeit a little haltingly. The newcomers 'tend to be admired, if sometimes grudgingly, for hard work and enterprise,' as one think tank put it.[93]

A lot of ink has been spilt on immigration under New Labour. For all the people heading to Britain to work or join their loved ones, the government didn't tie itself in knots over economic or family migration, or at least not when the economy was growing so healthily. But there was quickly a moral panic over people coming to Britain for another reason: the unprecedented number of men, women and children heading this way to ask for asylum. That is what we look at in detail in the next chapter.

# CHAPTER THREE
# HOW TO MAKE LIFE MISERABLE
# FOR REFUGEES

## A long tradition

In 1998, New Labour published a much-anticipated paper on immigration. While encouraging more people to make their lives in Britain, the government was determined not to appear 'soft' on any abuse of that generosity, and so the paper is packed with references to clampdowns and tough new proposals to keep immigrants in line. The paper also made the following promise on asylum and refugees:

> The UK has a long-standing tradition of giving shelter to those fleeing persecution in other parts of the world, and refugees in turn have contributed much to our society and culture. The Government is determined to uphold that tradition.[94]

They were bold words, from a government determined to do bold things. So let's meet some refugees, and the care and compassion they found when they turned to Britain for help.

## Returned to torture

Blaise Kamba came to the UK and asked for asylum in 2006. Kamba was 28, a young man who fled his home in the Democratic Republic of Congo (DRC) after local police arrested him over his political activities. It was an extremely dangerous time to come to the attention of the Congolese authorities: by this point 45,000 people were being killed every single month in the DRC amid a bloody, decade-long civil war, according to the International Rescue Committee.[95]

Kamba settled in Teesside and waited for a decision, only to be bundled into a plane and back to the DRC in 2008 when the Home Office decided he didn't qualify for sanctuary. Grim reports soon surfaced about what happened next. Kamba's friends, along with his local MP, confirmed that he had been taken from the airport by Congolese government officials as soon as his plane landed. In one of Kinshasa's most notorious interrogation centres, he was handcuffed, blindfolded and beaten, accused of being a spy and a traitor. British officials had declared he would be safe back home. He was not.[96]

Kamba was not the only one. Shortly afterwards journalists told more stories of Congolese asylum seekers who had been denied protection in Britain and who were then incarcerated and tortured immediately on return to the DRC. People who had asked for help here ended up back in Congolese prisons, beaten, burned and forced to drink their own urine.[97]

And our government? A Home Office spokesperson confirmed that ministers didn't even try to make sure asylum seekers were safe after being sent back into the depths of a civil war: 'We do not routinely monitor the treatment of individuals once removed from the UK.'

## Raped then called liars

For women in particular, the DRC could be hell. In 2010, one UN official called it 'the rape capital of the world.'[98]

Little surprise, then, that 80% of Congolese women asking for asylum in Britain told the Home Office that they had been raped. But the Home Office decided that these women were liars. Two-thirds of asylum claims going back to 2008 were rejected, and the women were told to return to the hell from which they had just fled.[99] 'The default setting for the UK Border Agency is that women who claim to have been raped are lying,' reported *The Guardian*.[100]

'I cannot forget them,' one victim would later tell a charity, recalling the attitude of the officials who rejected her claim. 'When I told them about my life they didn't believe me, and that hurt a lot.'

## Deported in agony

In 2008 a young man from Afghanistan, stuck in a detention centre after his refugee application was rejected and about to be removed from Britain, had a final plea. He was in no fit state to go anywhere: the braces on his teeth had become half detached, forcing the metal into his gums and leaving him in agony. Could he get his braces fixed before he was forced onto a plane?

The Home Office said no. His local MP got involved. Still no. Nothing must derail the scheduled removal. He was forced onto the plane regardless, denied the simple procedure which would have spared him pain. It was the sort of act of petty cruelty which asylum campaigners saw all the time.*

## Some definitions

The world of asylum and refugees has its own technocratic language, but it is relatively straightforward.

Someone who comes from outside Europe to ask for sanctuary in Britain is an asylum seeker. There is no visa to enter the country and do so, but anyone can ask for help once they are here. Through a lawyer, they present their story and whatever sup-

---

* This was the experience of one of the constituents helped by Jenny Willott MP when I worked for her.

porting documents they have to Home Office officials, who make a decision on their claim. If they are granted the right to stay in safety here, they become a refugee. If the government decides they don't meet the criteria for a refugee – of which more later – then asylum seekers can appeal that decision to a judge, who will either reverse the Home Office ruling or agree that this asylum seeker must return home.

It is a process with a lot at stake, and it has plenty of moving parts, with lawyers and charities and translators and international research all playing a role. But it isn't *that* complicated. So how did Britain end up sending people back to torture and rejecting so many women who had fled rape as a weapon of war?

The answer can be split broadly in two: immigration systems failing and, in a way which still feels shocking many years on, a noisy, national panic in the press and among politicians.

First, the systems.


## People on the move

The world since 1990 has been full of bloody conflict. Anyone turning on the evening news will have seen these global horrors unfold: the bafflingly complex conflict in the Balkans and the oppression of Kurds in Iraq; the continued brutal crackdown on women in Pakistan and the Somali civil war; genocides in Rwanda and the Sudan; the cruelty of governments in Afghanistan and Zimbabwe; bombs falling on civilians in Syria and the Yemen; torture in Eritrea.

The idea that Britain might be untouched by such turmoil is obviously fanciful. Millions of people have been forced to flee their homes, and while the majority try to find sanctuary in refugee camps on their own borders, many sought safety and security further away.

This isn't to say that people could just up and go to another country if they were in trouble. Tougher visa regimes (especially as the 2000s wore on) and stricter border controls saw to that. But moving around the world *was* easier.

The 90s heralded two revolutions, first in international travel and then in communications. In short, it suddenly became quicker and easier to get from country to country, while a mobile phone – and later a smart phone – eased the flow of information between people on the move and the friends or networks who could help them reach their destination.

Such journeys, by air and sea and trudging over land, were fraught with danger. And they cost serious money, which for some families meant taking on eye-watering debt to gangs of people smugglers, who flourished in number and promised to spirit them to a new, safer continent.

For some this meant Britain (in many years during the early 2000s, more people asked for sanctuary here than in any other EU country). Although the government soon started restricting visas from countries which produced a lot of asylum seekers, people nonetheless arrived and claimed sanctuary in unprecedented numbers, having either entered legally then asked for help or sneaked into the country. They placed their hopes in an asylum process which it turned out was woefully inadequate and quickly overwhelmed.

We shouldn't be naïve. Not everyone who asked for asylum was going to get it. People actively abused the process by applying under numerous identities or fabricating a tale of persecution, a betrayal of both the system and the people who were in obvious and grave danger. But many asylum seekers fell into a much greyer area, where they had good reason to fear their home countries yet it wasn't immediately clear what sort of obligation Britain had to them. It was complex and fraught work, but it should not have been beyond the wit of a modern government to find a fair and decent solution.

This is easier to guarantee when the numbers of people involved is relatively low, or is at least stable. Instead, asylum numbers were incredibly volatile.

During the 80s barely 4,000 people asked for asylum in Britain each year. That's around eleven people a day arriving in Britain and asking for sanctuary.[101]

But by 1991 asylum numbers had grown tenfold, to nearly 45,000 (see Figure 4). Those eleven requests each day swelled to one hundred and twenty.

Then numbers dropped sharply again. They halved to 22,000 in 1993; then started rising once more. There were just over 30,000 applications in 1997. It would be a decade before they dropped to this level again. By 2000, there were 80,000 asylum applications. We were up to two hundred and thirty claims each day.

And then the numbers suddenly plunged down again. They halved by 2003, then halved again by 2005. There were just 18,000 claims in 2010, the lowest number since the 80s. But it didn't last. The numbers started to rise steadily once more after that, back above 30,000 again by 2016.

The public, with some justification, thought the whole thing looked out of control.

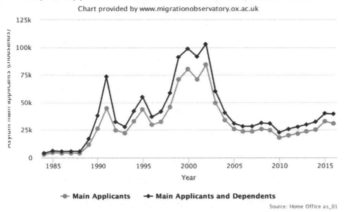

Figure 4. Source: Migration Observatory

## The rules

These sorts of spikes in numbers would have posed a challenge to most administrative systems. But it wasn't just the numbers which caused problems.

The international rules on how to look after refugees are hopelessly out of date. The Refugee Convention was finalised in 1951, shaped and influenced by the years after the Second World War. Even if the key principle is simple – 'Refugees are people who cannot safely go home,' as the former foreign secretary David Miliband puts it in his book *Rescue*[102] – the Convention inevitably reflects the period when it was written. Looking back to the Holocaust and forward to the Cold War, it is very clear on protecting people in danger because of their religion, nationality, race or political beliefs, but this leaves an awful lot of gaps when thinking about to-day's refugees. No one in 1951 could have imagined what a refugee crisis might look like in the twen-ty-first century: millions of people fleeing for their lives, facing forms of violence that would not have crossed the minds of serious jurists in Geneva in the 50s. Some modern-day refugees have been targeted directly by murderous governments; many will be saving their families from indiscriminate bombings and murders in their towns and villages; some are in terror not of the state but of their own families and communities, in countries where the police are either complicit in abuse or non-existent. Some will have been raped, or tortured, or trafficked. They may have been targeted for supporting the wrong political party or loving the wrong person or being the wrong sex. The Home Office, confronted with modern life at its most horrific, could only draw on seriously out-of-date legislation.*

No wonder people got lost in the process; no wonder decisions were delayed or wrong or never made at all. It is hardly a surprise that the system felt the strain. What no one could have guessed was the extent of this collapse.

---

* One obvious solution would be to renegotiate a whole new set of rules better suited to the present day, but refugee advocates are understandably nervous that this would give politicians the chance to restrict refugee rights even further. We are likely to be stuck with the Refugee Convention for many years to come.

## Mind-blowing

As the number of asylum applications ratcheted-up in the mid-90s, the Home Office opened shiny new offices in south London, in theory to bring a smoother, more efficient approach to the immigration process, including asylum. Ministers claimed the new system and computer programmes were state of the art.

They were not. When Barbara Roache took over as one of Tony Blair's first immigration ministers in 1999, she found fewer than fifty civil servants trained and in post to handle asylum cases. There were nowhere near enough officials to make decisions quickly and fairly.[103] Asylum applications began to mount up. Then the IT system failed. It was fixed – and promptly failed again.

By 2000 (the year when a peak of over 80,000 asylum seekers asked for help) 'there were almost fifteen miles of unshelved paperwork waiting to be investigated; letters went astray; phones went unanswered,' according to Robert Winder. Anyone asking for sanctuary at this time was entering a 'morass of queues, lost files, hesitant decisions and unenforceable rulings.' Wilder concluded: 'The system, if that is the right word for something so disorderly, was failing.'[104]

Asylum seekers were sent to live in hostels after they had asked for help, were interviewed shortly afterwards about the reasons they had fled home, and then dispatched to temporary housing to wait to hear their fate – and wait and wait. It wasn't unusual for decisions to take months or even years.

The majority of asylum seekers were told – eventually – that they didn't qualify to stay as refugees. Thousands of people then left Britain, under their own steam or escorted onto planes by government officials; but tens of thousands more either put in new asylum claims with a few extra details to boost the original argument and joined the back of the queue all over again, or they slipped off the Home Office radar entirely.

Oona King, a leading Labour MP under Blair, described what it was like trying to help constituents whose applications had been swallowed up in this machine. She would take up a case with a minister, she explained:

> This civil servant told me that they write letters to people saying the home secretary has 'seen the correspondence'. Apparently, they wheel thousands of letters past his desk on a trolley. [...] When the home secretary gives the wheelbarrow a once over, they can truthfully state that he has seen the correspondence.

'The apocryphal and the mundane blend together at the Home Office like absinthe,' King wrote in her diary. 'It blows your mind.'[105]

In purely bureaucratic terms you can understand the size of the task. Maybe you can even forgive the number of things which went wrong. What you can't defend is how officials and politicians reacted.

## Home Office culture: 'they all lie'

The Home Office officials tasked with looking at asylum cases are making life and death decisions. From the depths of his prison cell back in the DRC, Blaise Kamba could testify to the seriousness of getting these decisions right. And yet the Home Office wasn't simply overwhelmed. Its whole culture was rotten.

Officials routinely, callously dismissed asylum seekers as liars. This was not the same as patiently testing evidence and personal stories to make sure they stacked up. It was the systemic assumption that someone pleading for safety in Britain was fibbing, even before that person had opened their mouth.

'They all lie,' according to one civil servant, quoted in research by a team of immigration experts. 'In her long career,' the experts wrote, this official claimed she had 'never met an asylum seeker she believed.'[106]

Or there is the official who blew the whistle on behaviour in the Cardiff branch of the Home Office in 2010, disgusted at what she witnessed. On her first day on the job, a manager told her 'if it was up to me I'd take them outside and shoot them,' reported *The Guardian*. The office mascot was a stuffed toy gorilla, tossed from desk to desk as a badge of shame for anyone who granted refugee status to an asylum seeker. (A subsequent internal investigation decided there was nothing racist about the gorilla). 'I witnessed general hostility, rudeness and indifference towards clients,' the whistle-blower explained. 'It was completely horrific. I highlighted my concerns to senior managers but they just laughed at me.'[107]

This racism was implicit, just about, but elsewhere it was wholly explicit. 'I remember one caseworker complaining that her village was 'full of Pakis',' another former asylum official wrote in an article for the BBC website. 'When I asked her if she thought she was in the right job, she replied, 'Yes, because I've got a chance to stop more coming in'.'[108]

The results were predictable. In this period the Home Office rejected thousands of people who did, in fact, need help and protection. The charity Asylum Aid has crunched a decade of data on asylum decisions.[109] They looked at what happened when cases refused by the Home Office then came before an appeal judge. The findings are damning.

The government has got at least one in four of its asylum refusals wrong every single year since 2007 (for women) and every year but one since 2010 (for men). A staggering 40% of *all* refusals were wrong in 2016. To put this another way: the Home Office consistently got 25% of its decisions wrong, year after year after year, yet has still managed to get even worse. In any other part of the legal system these sorts of numbers would be a national disgrace.

Here was a different kind of evidence that the system had collapsed. Asylum seekers were throwing themselves on the mercy of the British state, and were trusting their lives to a system which was riven with failures, plagued by delays and, it turned out, host to a smattering of racists as well.

While the official system creaked and asylum seekers suffered, the press had a field day.

## What the papers say

It is difficult to exaggerate the media frenzy that arose around asylum in these years. Researchers have catalogued how asylum seekers were described in mainstream press stories from the late-90s to the mid-2000s, and it is depressing reading.

'Asylum tide costs Britain £2bn a year' (*Sunday Times*, 1998); 'Asylum seekers are revolting' (*Star*, 2000); 'Widow, 88, told by GP: make way for asylum seekers' (*Daily Mail*, 2003); 'Asylum killer on the loose' (*Daily Express*, 2003); and so the list goes on, for pages and pages.[110] The statistics are extraordinary. As we heard in the introduction, in a single month during 2002 the *Daily Express* ran twenty-two frontpage stories about asylum seekers. There were 1,961 stories about asylum seekers in mainstream British newspapers in 2006, and even though this dropped over time there were still 1,351 asylum stories in 2011. It is hard to compare these numbers with coverage of other issues, but at one point someone picking up a copy of the *Mail* or the *Express* would find that a quarter of the stories inside were about asylum in some way.[111]

The press gorged on these sorts of articles. The sheer number of stories can be explained partly by the editorial instincts of Fleet Street bosses, some of whom were personally unhappy about immigration, but much more important was the perfect tabloid ingredients that asylum stories offered: government systems falling apart, heroes and (more often) villains, a Little Englander despair at a world spinning out of control. They were irresistible.

It wasn't that they never had merit as stories (although some, as we shall see, definitely did not) so much that it created a clamour of negative noise around asylum seekers. By the time the BBC started to give it serious attention for radio and TV, asylum coverage had gone mainstream.

As quickly as the press could dream up problems, asylum seekers were offered as scapegoats. They were associated with stealing the identities of dead children, pushing up Council Tax, making a mockery of British justice, creating water shortages, even stealing and eating donkeys. They were a 'time bomb', 'scroungers', 'parasites' and – a word which quickly came to dominate media stories about asylum – 'bogus'.

The most famous front page of all is the one about asylum seekers killing and cooking the Queen's swans. This was in the *Sun* in July 2003 (Figure 5), and alleged that 'callous eastern European' asylum seekers had baited some traps, caught a swan and then roasted it for a barbeque. The police 'swooped' to put a stop to what the paper called a 'regular' occurrence.[112]

It is memorable stuff. It is also a work of fiction from beginning to end.

Figure 5. Source: UNHCR

The freelance journalist Nick Medic, fed up with seeing asylum seekers abused in the papers and suspicious about the failure to name the supposed swan-eaters (standard practice in a story about police arrests), tirelessly traced the roots of the story.

It became clear that the *Sun*'s story was about an event for which it had no evidence, misquoted its only source, reported arrests which never took place, and cited a 'report' into foreigners eating swans which turned out to be an internal memo with no reference to anyone of any nationality eating anything at all.[113]

The story should have failed even the most basic editorial test for accuracy and truthfulness. Instead it was published on the front page. It confirmed prejudices about asylum seekers that the press had been peddling for years, and this was more than enough to get it past the editors. This was fake news long before Donald Trump gave it its name.

## Turning refugees into criminals

Under pressure, successive governments piled bad laws onto failing systems, in a desperate attempt both to tighten control over asylum and be seen to get tough on something which was splashed all over the press and starting to worry voters. Ministers decided, yet again, to get hostile.

Harsher and harsher legislation treated asylum seekers not as people in fear but as criminals-in-waiting. It wasn't just that proposals for dealing with asylum started to resemble promises to deal with crime, but that the ambient noise around asylum was now dominated by talk of legal restrictions and new ways to punish people. Everything to do with asylum and refugees suddenly seemed on the wrong side of the law.

It started in 1996. The Asylum and Immigration Act became law in the last throes of John Major's Conservative government, and it is a template for many of the New Labour 'clampdowns' on asylum which followed. 'The idea,' Winder writes, 'was to deter asylum-seekers partly by making their lives even more miserable, and partly by punishing anyone who helped them, even if they did so unwittingly.'[114] Merely helping someone who went on to claim asylum – whether you knew they were going to do so or not – could get you into trouble.

The message wasn't terribly subtle. Asylum seekers were bad news, and were best avoided. They were out to hoodwink ordinary members of the public. If we all gave asylum seekers a wide berth, we would be better off. It was grim stuff, but much worse was to follow.

Thus we got the 1999 Immigration and Asylum Act. Asylum seekers were now dispersed all over the country after making a claim (this was a sensible move to try and relieve one or two local councils burdened with looking after thousands of people every year, but in practice it meant carting asylum seekers off to run-down estates around the country where they knew no one). They were taken off mainstream benefits and moved onto a parallel system of vouchers ('a humiliating procedure which more or less branded the recipients as imposters,' says Winder).[115]

Then came the 2002 Nationality, Immigration and Asylum Act, which expanded the number of supposedly safe countries to which asylum seekers could be shipped off without an appeal hearing. This so-called 'white list' of countries now included Albania, which meant sex trafficking victims could be returned to the country at the very centre of Europe's trafficking networks. It is hard to imagine anywhere more dangerous to send them.

The 2002 Act was supposed to be New Labour's sweeping final word on asylum, its decisive clampdown, but they were back less than two years later with the Asylum and Immigration (Treatment of Claimants, etc) Act. This threatened to remove even basic financial support from refused asylum seekers, and punished anyone who claimed asylum but didn't hold legitimate identity documents. As usual there was some logic here – doubtless some people did destroy their papers, in the belief that they would then be harder to remove from Britain – but above all it was a gift to criminal gangs. People traffickers already routinely took passports from their victims, as one measure to control them. The government had just handed them another advantage: a threat of arrest, detention and deportation now hung over any trafficking victim who escaped and asked for help. New Labour's Home Office, where the government was famously proud to be tough on crime and tough on the causes of crime, had actively given criminal gangs the upper hand in their brutal exploitation of sex slaves. It was unforgivable.

## Actual crime

All of which begs the legitimate and obvious question: were immigrants, and asylum seekers in particular, responsible for waves of crime up and down the country in the early part of the 2000s? Could the government point to this as some justification?

The short answer is, No. Tom Gash, a crime expert who at one time worked under Blair, has already demolished this myth. Research into EU immigration after 2004 shows that 'areas with higher immigration did not experience more crime. They had roughly the same levels of violent crime as those with low immigration,' wrote Gash. 'And there was in fact *less* property crime in places where there had been a larger A8 influx [that is, the EU countries granted access to Britain after 2004, minus Cyprus

and Malta]. This is a striking finding and contradicted warnings from some segments of the media.'
And asylum seekers? Gash notes a 'slight increase' in
property crime and 'no real change' in violent crime
in areas where asylum seekers had been sent to live,
compared to other parts of Britain.[116]

We shouldn't pretend that the slight increase
doesn't exist or matter, but neither should we imagine it justifies a decade of screaming headlines
and swingeing new laws. Local police already have
perfectly sensible plans for dealing with areas where
there is slightly more crime, from putting more
cops on the beat to running crime prevention ses-
sions. Along with the rest of us, neighbourhood
cops would probably have benefitted if politicians
in the 2000s had responded less to hysteria and more
to the facts on the ground.

The facts on the ground can change, of course.
Recent studies in Germany and Sweden *have* linked
larger asylum seeker populations with higher
crime.[117] We should keep a close eye on what the
data tells us and make decisions accordingly – but
let's not pretend there was any justification for all
that noise at the beginning of the millennium link-
ing asylum seekers, refugees and crime. There was
none.

## The government mindset

David Blunkett was the Labour Home Secretary between 2001 and 2004. Throughout his time in government, Blunkett kept a diary, and in summer 2001 he records in passing a chat he has had with the Prime Minister.

'Tony [Blair] wants no asylum seekers entering the country', Blunkett notes, then promptly moves on.[118] A brief mention perhaps, but it is a mind-boggling sentence. Two of Britain's most powerful men had been talking about closing the border entirely to people fleeing murder and violence. It would have been against international law, let alone Britain's moral obligations to the world. Thousands of people would have been abandoned to death and violence. The knock-on effect for other countries spooked by asylum could have been catastrophic. Buoyed by the British decision, who else would have shut their borders as the world burned?

It is only a short sentence, though. Maybe it was mentioned only as an aside, barely a serious suggestion at all. Or, more alarmingly, maybe the Home Secretary of the day didn't think that the fact this suggestion was being made at all merited too much reflection. Maybe, chillingly, we had reached the point where the idea of turning torture victims away from safety just wasn't that big a deal.

## Moving on

Gradually, as asylum numbers dropped away, the attention of politicians and reporters moved on. Gordon Brown, having taken over from Tony Blair in 2007, made no major speeches on asylum and made no substantial changes to the law. Brown did get caught on a rogue microphone accusing a voter of being a 'bigoted woman' after she had raised some pretty mild complaints about immigration with him, but for all the hand-wringing it provoked even this incident made little impact on public opinion.[119] A decade of noise and fury faded away.

But it left its scars. When refugees started heading for Europe in large numbers again a few years later, the press eased back into its old role. Politicians panicked once more. We will look at this much more in chapter five. For now, a new government had its own ideas about getting tough on immigration, and it was prepared to bring a whole new level of hostility to public life in doing so.

## CHAPTER FOUR
# THERESA MAY FROM THE HOME OFFICE

### 'Go home'

One Enoch Powell speech in May 1965 – three years before Rivers of Blood but rehearsing many of the same ideas – was greeted with an approving *Daily Mail* headline the next morning: 'POWELL'S SEND THEM HOME PLAN.'[120]

As the *Mail*'s headline-writers would have known perfectly well, it is the sort of language which had been used to terrorise immigrants for years. *Go home, send them back*: it was all part of the anti-immigrant rhetoric which had flourished over the decades.

Zip forward to summer 2013 and the same words were back in the political mainstream. The Home Office, at that point under the stewardship of Theresa May, approved a scheme to mount billboards on the backs of vans across London, emblazoned with the words GO HOME OR FACE ARREST. In case this was too subtle, the poster included a picture of a pair of handcuffs along with the number of immigrants in the local area who had been arrested. There was a telephone line to text for advice on leaving Britain.

The media called the whole initiative the Go Home Vans, and the name stuck. For a couple of months, it felt as if every news broadcast and opinion piece looked at the Go Home Vans from a fresh angle: had the Home Office gone too far; would anyone actually use the number (apart from pranksters); would the vans just stay in London or would they tour the whole nation?

More facts soon emerged. The Home Office spent less than £10,000 on the project (an infinitesimal total from an annual budget of more than £10 billion). Hardly anyone *did* leave the country after seeing the vans (sixty people, according to the government; eleven, according to campaigners). The Immigration Minister confirmed later that year that the Go Home Vans had been scrapped and wouldn't be coming back.[121]

It had been a failure. Or had it?

Like the *Daily Mail* all those decades before, Theresa May and her officials knew the impact of putting this vocabulary into common circulation. It was targeted at illegal (or irregular) immigrants, May insisted. A clutch of research after 2010 showed that voters wanted the government to focus on tackling illegal immigration, and there is certainly a fair argument that, given the strength of public feeling, the government had a mandate or even a responsibility to find solutions.

This is the background, but it isn't any justification for what the government decided to do next. May and her team understood the likely impact of the language. It was a way to frighten a new generation of immigrants in Britain, just as the generation before them had been frightened. It was aimed at making the British state into something they feared and making them think twice about building their lives here.

By these measures, the vans had worked. For a tiny investment, news of the vans had spread far and wide, through traditional and social media, and had certainly reached the eyes and ears of thousands of migrants. The public had heard about (yet another) crackdown. For immigrants themselves, life had been made that little bit less pleasant.

The vans were just the opening shots in a whole new plan to exert more pressure on immigrants in Britain, co-opting teachers, doctors and even charities in the latest efforts to get tough on immigration. The government even gave the plan a name, for the first time naming in public what politicians had been quietly trying to create for years: the 'hostile environment.'

Shamefully, ministers were proud of policies designed to make Britain a less welcoming place. But, while they may not have realised it at the time, they had also unleashed a policy they could not control. When that realisation came, it came with a bang.

## Open hostility

After the 2010 General Election, the Conservatives found they had backed themselves into a corner.

The party had come up with a rather neat-looking campaign promise on immigration: a Tory government would bring down net immigration to the 'tens of thousands.' Any analysis of the cap would have shown the serious risk it posed to the British economy, but the motivation behind the policy was purely political. It was developed to win votes by tapping into public anxiety through a commitment which was clear, memorable and measurable. It went down a storm on the doorstep.

But it quickly proved very difficult to achieve in government, not least because it depended on things ministers couldn't control. This was all pre-Brexit, so they couldn't stop EU citizens entering the country. Neither could ministers dictate how many people left Britain. There was no simple, single lever anyone in power could pull to honour what was, in fact, a very complex promise. The tens-of-thousands policy was far, far messier than it first seemed, and it was failing. After an early drop in numbers, net immigration was above 200,000 again by 2013.

Theresa May and the Home Office were not even close to giving voters what she had promised.

The 'hostile environment' emerged as the government scrambled for more creative ways to drag the numbers down, mainly by making Britain less attractive to new and existing immigrants. The outcome was creative all right. It was also deeply unpleasant.

As we have already seen, politicians in a panic often reach for new legislation. May was no different. She steered through a whole raft of legal changes in the 2014 Immigration Act, which restricted the rights of immigrants across the most basic areas of their lives. Unlike previous regimes, though, this wasn't aimed at controlling the borders but squarely at people already living here. The idea that this would only affect illegal immigrants was entirely implausible, not least because it was at the strategic heart of attempts to meet the tens-of-thousands promise, which was aimed entirely at *legal* migration.

The list of new rules was chilling. It dictated where someone could live, who they could marry, and how they looked after their health. And it moved the frontline of immigration control away from the government and deep into society, with sanctions hanging over businesses and public bodies which didn't co-operate.

Private landlords now had to check the immigration status of potential tenants; employers had to check additional documents before offering people work; immigrants would have to pay an extra tax towards the NHS as part of applying to come to Britain, re-enforcing the lie that migrants are a burden, rather than a boon, to the public purse; banks were told to run background checks against immigrants who wanted to open accounts; officials could now revoke driving licenses based on immigration status; the Home Office would have greater direct powers over whether or not immigrants could get married; and immigration enforcement officers were given more police-like powers to stop and search.[122]

The whole list makes for unhappy reading. Ordinary workers were told to become an advance battalion of border guards. These new laws compelled citizens to work alongside the Home Office in monitoring the people they encountered every day or, at worst, actually to do the government's dirty work themselves.

It appalled commentators on Britain's liberal left – but it was also anathema to the libertarian instincts of UKIP, who hardly hold a beacon to high immigration. As the party's former spin doctor Gawain Towler put it: 'We don't believe that publicans, licensees, shop keepers, hotel owners should be security guards, should be made into the border force.

We pay our taxes for *you* [politicians] to sort that out.'[123] Here again there is a strong sense that the British public took a far more decent approach to immigration than politicians supposed.

Not that this gave May reason to pause. Having overseen this sort of political strategy at the Home Office, she simply pursued it with extra vigour once she reached 10 Downing Street.

## Mrs May at Number 10

One of the great paradoxes about Theresa May is that, for all her instinctive harshness towards Britain's immigrants, she has a genuine feel for injustice in other parts of society.

Her speech in July 2016, delivered from the steps outside Downing Street as the new Prime Minister, made a heartfelt appeal to those in Britain who were getting by but were worried about what the future held. Commentators more or less agreed that her commitment to Brits who are 'just-about-managing' (quickly christened the 'JAMs') was genuine.

'I know you're working around the clock,' she said, addressing the JAMs directly. 'I know you are doing your best, and I know that sometimes life can be a struggle. The government I lead will be driven not by the interests of the privileged few, but by yours.'[124]

It is a good speech and a fine sentiment. But her keynote hostile immigration policies, started at the Home Office and resurrected as Prime Minister, didn't just make life harder and more complex for immigrants. It also hit British workers in frontline jobs.

The burden for managing immigration fell on the sort of public sector JAMs May had promised to help. Teaching assistants, overworked civil servants and NHS administrators who already, justifiably, wanted to know why their pay had been frozen for five years, were now being told to do extra, unsavoury work with no obvious reward. People fed-up with the government and stretched to breaking point were given more to do. They had been promised help but felt like they were being punished. It was unpleasant policy and rubbish politics (and possibly a window into the sort of mistakes which cost May a majority in the snap 2017 General Election).

Seemingly blind to all this, though, May proceeded to crank-up the 'hostile environment' a series more notches. The extra pressure didn't impress those frontline staff – who flocked to Jeremy Corbyn at that snap election – and it deepened the misery for immigrants. The lengths the government would go in vain pursuit of its arbitrary immigration cap was genuinely shocking.

First came more demands on doctors and nurses. In January 2017 the Home Office convinced NHS officials to share its data on patients. In the dry words of the formal deal struck between the two departments, healthcare data could now be used for 'tracing immigration offenders.' In practice it was a stitch-up between Health Minister Jeremy Hunt and Home Secretary Amber Rudd, to make the NHS a more potent weapon in Theresa May's immigration clampdown.[125]

In October 2017 the demands were expanded still further, and doctors were asked to make 'reasonable enquiries' on the immigration status of patients. This was ostensibly to check whether patients owed the new up-front fees now charged to some immigrants, but inevitably it generated more databases which were shared directly with the Home Office.

Then there were additional rules for schools. From June 2016 – the month in which the country voted for Brexit and May's campaign to be Prime Minister rolled into action – schools had been asked to collect more data on children, including their nationality and country of birth, and told to pass this on to other government agencies (including May's Home Office). Another dry deal in Whitehall, which in this case led to schools sharing details of more than 18,000 families with the Home Office in a single year, including names, addresses and how often children turned up to lessons.

But even this was 'a watered-down version of a far more draconian project initiated by May when she was home secretary,' according to the journalists Nathalie Bloomer and Samir Jeraj. Back in 2015 May had tried (and failed) to introduce plans which would essentially have barred children from going to school at all if their families were in the country illegally. At the time May's cabinet colleagues had blocked her, arguing that immigration enforcement had no place 'in the emotive issue of children's education,' but May came back to the whole issue once in Downing Street.[126]

Charities co-operated with the Home Office, too. Through a system which only pays voluntary organisations if they hit targets set by public bodies, some homeless charities were rewarded with cash not for rehoming European citizens but for referring them to the Home Office for deportation. By 2015 those rewards were explicitly linked to how many homeless EU nationals were removed from Britain.[127] The anti-immigrant agenda had made inroads into the voluntary sector, a bit of British society supposedly there to keep ministers in check.

It gets worse. In March 2017 a woman visited a London police station to report that she had been kidnapped and raped. Officers referred her to a charity specialising in care for victims of sexual assault – only for the police to return later, arrest her, and drag her back to a police station for questioning over her immigration status. The police had been expected to help enforce the hostile environment – cops and immigration officials worked together more closely than ever under May – and there had long been fears that immigrants wouldn't report crime for fear of how they would be treated. Here was shocking proof that these fears were well-founded.[128]

Reporters uncovered one more gruesome detail: it seemed likely that Members of Parliament had been shopping their own constituents to the Home Office for removal. Four hundred and eighty-two immigration tip-offs had come from MPs between 2014 and 2016, using a dedicated government telephone hotline and website.[129] For some immigrants, a visit to the local MP is the only way to get clear help and advice amid all the chaos created by the Home Office. The betrayal of trust is horrifying.*

## Trawling

The public was, at best, dimly aware of the things being done in the name of the hostile environment. But that was about to change.

* I worked as an MP's caseworker for nearly four years between 2006 and 2010. While there is no formal agreement of what an MP should do for his or her constituents, it would have been unthinkable for us – or any of the other MPs and staff I knew – to report someone to the immigration authorities if they had come to our office for help.

Immigration charities – at least, those not contracted to help kick migrants out of the country – had been warning the Home Office in private for years that these policies would have a sweeping impact not just on legal and illegal migrants but also on any British citizens who didn't have the right documents to prove their nationality. This is a surprisingly large number of people, they pointed out, and raised cases of British citizens who, when they couldn't produce the documents now demanded by the Home Office, were billed thousands of pounds for free NHS care or lost their jobs. The *Guardian* newspaper picked up the theme, and by the start of 2018 it was publishing stories about some of those people: the Jamaican-born man told to pay £58,000 for cancer treatment, the British guy from Islington who left Antigua as a child in the 50s yet was told he would be deported back there. Why, the articles asked, was the Home Office targeting 'a large group of Black Caribbean men and women who have been here since the 1960s'?[130]

Officials continued to deny there were any problems, but in March the *Guardian* had another story: representatives from Britain's former colonies, in London for a meeting of commonwealth leaders, had asked to talk to the Home Office about the effect of the 'hostile environment' and had been turned down. Ministers looked ridiculous. British citizens were being punished by immigration policies which should never have touched their lives, and the government was turning away diplomats who wanted to find out why.

More stories emerged. It turned out British citizens from *Windrush* families had been deported because they didn't have the right documents (sixty-three in total). More had ended up stuck in the Caribbean because they had travelled on holiday then weren't allowed back into Britain, missing weddings and funerals back home. Thousands had been denied healthcare, thrown out of their jobs and flung into detention centres. Some British citizens who had lived here for decades were too frightened to contact the Home Office to clarify their immigration status, in fear that officials would then come after them.

The public was appalled. Ironically, given the scepticism and violence which met Caribbean families in Britain in the 70s and 80s, by the millennium these same families were seen as a valuable part of British history, credited with powering the post-war jobs boom and helping build the NHS. People were angry and baffled: why on earth was the government picking on men and women who had done so much for the country?[131]

The Home Secretary – Amber Rudd, who succeeded Theresa May – eventually resigned after weeks of scrutiny (not because of the policies, which were May's initiatives, but because under relentless pressure she ended up misleading parliament about targets for deporting migrants from Britain). Nonetheless, the government continued to defend the hostile environment. The mistreatment of *Windrush* families was an administrative error, they insisted, one which could be fixed so that British nationals would no longer get caught up in policies targeted at illegal immigrants.

But this was nonsense. The hostile environment is best understood as a big net, trawling society to see who, when seeing a doctor or applying for a driving license or trying to get a job, has the right documents and who does not. As those charities had warned it was inevitable that British citizens would end up dragged into the net as well, with tragic consequences.

Some of the initiatives mentioned in previous pages were rolled-back. Home Office access to NHS on immigrants was tightened again, and schools were told that they no longer had to collect nationality data on children. Ministers still defended the hostile environment, though. They repeated the argument that the *Windrush* scandal was a glitch in a system otherwise geared to catch illegal migrants, rather than a system so sweeping and so flawed that this sort of scandal was inevitable. They were so addicted to hostile policies that they simply closed their eyes to the glaring errors and the wrecked lives.

## Lock 'em up

One aspect of the hostile environment survived intact, in all its horror. Like successive Labour Home Secretaries, Theresa May was enthusiastic about putting immigrants in prison.

This isn't a question of jailing immigrants for committing crimes through the same justice system as everyone else but of locking them up in a parallel (and relatively little-known) system saved solely for immigrants. Whole books could be written about this, but for now the broad details paint their own grim picture.

Ministers have had the power to imprison immigrants since the 70s, provided that officials are in the final stage of removing from the country someone who has no right to be here. In practice, even this rule is constantly breached, given that the majority of people are not removed but, eventually, released back into their communities.

This tiny corner of government business has grown sixteen-fold in forty years. Two hundred and fifty dedicated spaces have expanded to 4,000 today, spread across eleven Immigration Detention Centres. Over the course of a year, the government can and does imprison 30,000 immigrants, from people who have overstayed their visas, to asylum seekers who have exhausted any right to stay here. And once an immigrant disappears into the network of detention centres, no one knows how long they will be there. Britain is the only country in Europe which places no time limit on detention.[132] The latest data shows that dozens of people have been held for a year or even longer, with no sign of removal and no promise of release.[133]

The government has long argued that detention and prison are not the same. But the people who see the system up-close aren't fooled. Here is what one Nigerian asylum seeker told the journalist Emily Dugan: 'It's called immigration detention but to me it's a prison: the high fences, the guards, the keys. How is it different from a prison?'[134] And here is Kate Osamor, a Labour MP, describing her own visit to one of these shady facilities: 'As you enter, you are asked for identification and a proof of address. You leave all your belongings in a locker. You are searched thoroughly... You queue and queue. It quickly becomes clear that you are visiting a prison'.[135] Ben Gelbium, a writer for The New Economic website, describes buildings 'hidden away in remote Victorian ex-prisons or behind barbed wire at the back of industrial estates.'[136] They are physically and politically shielded from public scrutiny: MPs complain that they are blocked from visiting the centres, and the private companies running most of them can hide even basic information behind confidentiality rules.

But we do know how dangerous they are. According to the charity Inquest, thirty-three people died in these centres between 2000 and 2017, with 2017 the deadliest year so far.[137] One centre, Yarl's Wood in Bedfordshire, was declared 'not safe' by inspectors in 2003; another, Brook House near Gatwick Airport, was described as 'fundamentally unsafe' by regulators in 2010. Both are still in use. Undercover journalists found racism and abuse rife among the private security guards working there; women have reported sexual abuse and intimidation.[138] Two detention centres are run as high-security prisons, even though its inmates are immigrants not violent criminals.

It is a stark reminder that some of the cruellest steps towards a hostile environment for immigrants were in place long before Theresa May took over. She simply pulled the whole thing together.

## The all-powerful Theresa May

Christopher Jackson has aptly described May's Home Office as 'a fiefdom committed to the promotion of her own values.'[139] These values continued with her into Downing Street. So how was she able to get away with it?

It is difficult to exaggerate how powerful a role Theresa May has had in British politics since 2010. The two main sources of political opposition had, in different ways, gone missing. She has had the whole field to herself.

The Liberal Democrats have traditionally had a much more tolerant approach to immigration, but they formed a coalition government with the Tories, which ran from 2010 to 2015. This allowed the Lib Dems to force through one extremely progressive and welcome change to immigration policy, with a huge reduction (if not a complete end) to putting children in immigration detention centres. Around 1,100 children were locked up in 2009, the final full year of a Labour government. This number was down to seventy-one in 2016.[140]

But as important as this was – and as life-changing as it was for children who would otherwise have spent time behind bars – this was where Lib Dem influence over May and immigration policy stuttered to a halt. In theory, the Lib Dems had a junior minister in the Home Office to keep an eye on May, but the Go Home Vans and the rest of the 'hostile environment' went ahead regardless. May's team told journalists that if Lib Dems in the department weren't onside then she would just make decisions without asking them.

In the meantime, the Labour Party under Ed Miliband found its own way to make things worse. Trapped between party activists who were pretty comfortable about immigration and a core vote deeply worried about it, Labour mainly fudged the whole question, but occasionally blundered into its own moments of scapegoating immigrants.

In a major speech in March 2013, for example, Shadow Home Secretary Yvette Cooper announced that Labour would make it a little harder for EU citizens to claim jobseekers' allowance, and would close the (admittedly crazy) loophole which meant child tax credits could be paid on behalf of kids who didn't actually live in Britain.

So far, so underwhelming. The most eye-catching pledge, though, was to make sure 'there should be stronger English language requirements on people who want to work in public services.' It was a throwaway line, but it had been promoted heavily in advance as a sign that Labour was ready to toughen up. The British public would no longer have to put up with council staff who couldn't speak English.[141]

But this promise was rubbish. There was (and is) zero evidence that public sector staff struggle with spoken English. If Brits couldn't get help with housing or tax or health because frontline staff couldn't speak English that *would* be a disgrace – but the problem didn't exist. The speech gave a public platform to a baseless piece of immigration-blaming, and re-enforced existing public concerns about a shortage of housing and public services.*

It was a speech designed to attack Theresa May and the Conservatives, but it was more likely to remind the then Home Secretary of why her position was so secure. May's political instincts against immigrants and immigration were as tough as we have seen, and her political opponents either joined in with her rhetoric or went missing in action. Even when the *Windrush* scandal exposed the cruelty of her policies, it was not May who lost her job but the colleague who followed her into the Home Office. She probably couldn't believe her luck.

## The next crisis

May spent six years at the Home Office, the longest tenure of modern times. She certainly offered greater stability than her predecessors during New

---

* Cooper quietly forgot these previous arguments and became a key critic of hostile environment policies when the *Windrush* scandal exposed them to public and parliament.

Labour's time in charge, which saw six Home Secretaries shuffled in and out of the post over thirteen years.

But May was also blindsided at the Home Office by developments which started thousands of miles away and swiftly reached mainland Europe. By 2011, amid renewed violence and terror especially in Africa and the middle east, more and more people were fleeing their homes. Realisation soon dawned that millions of desperate people were on the move, a substantial number of whom were willing to risk everything to get to the safety of Europe. Migrants were facing a desperate scrabble for survival, and modern Britain was about to be tested with yet another set of questions about immigration.

# CHAPTER FIVE
# THINKING ABOUT EUROPE

## Hell

It was July 2011, and Pietro Bartolo had grown used to helping migrants as they landed on the tiny Italian island of Lampedusa. He was, and still is, the island's doctor, and for months he had been looking after migrants crammed onto the boats which left Libya's northern shore and arrived on his island.

Even calling them boats is a bit generous. There were some larger vessels, but people arriving each year on this obscure outpost of Europe, one hundred and seventy miles from Sicily, were often stuffed onto small wooden crafts or dinghies. By 2011 there were already thousands of them, people risking the seas to flee a toxic mix of persecution, war, global warming and poverty across the middle east and north and central Africa. The boats were over-loaded with people from countries which had been rocked by conflict or destitution: Syrians, Libyans, Eritreans, Iraqis, Somalis, Afghans, Pakistanis, and countless others besides.*

Even so, nothing could have prepared Bartolo for what confronted him that morning. It haunted his dreams for years.

* Commentators have variously referred to this as both a refugee crisis and a migration crisis. People were on the move for a variety of reasons so I will use the latter.

Migrants often emerged from crossings confused and dehydrated. There were always traumatised children to check over and keep warm. But this
time something was different. The passengers didn't
look confused, they looked distraught. There was a
'problem in the hold,' someone told the doctor, so
Bartolo ducked into the pitch-black bowels of the
boat to see what was going on. It turned out that
this wasn't the hold but a storage freezer, once used
for keeping fish:

> The floor lit up, and I found myself in a chamber of
> hell. The hold was paved entirely with corpses. I had
> been walking on dead bodies. Innumerable young
> bodies. They were naked, piled on top of each other,
> some with limbs intertwined. It was Dantesque. The
> walls were scratched and dripping with blood. Many
> of the young dead people had no fingernails.[142]

This wasn't a seen from Dante's *Inferno*, though. It
was real life in twenty-first century Europe.

The facts emerged slowly from traumatised passengers. There were far too many people on the
boat, which was hardly unusual as the more people the smugglers could cram onto each voyage the
greater the profits they could make. In this case, the
boat was in danger of capsizing soon after setting
out, so the smugglers had forced people deep into

the hold to try and maintain its stability. Stuffed into a confined space with no air, they started to suffocate. Other passengers were forced at gunpoint to sit on the hatch, blocking the only way out. After clawing for hours at the walls to escape, two dozen people died.

It is hard to imagine a more harrowing scene, but huge numbers of boats were setting out and tragedies were widespread. 2011 was actually relatively quiet, compared with the years which followed. By 2015, 150,000 people a year were taking rickety boats to try and sail from Libya to Italy.[143] This wasn't the only route: in the same year, 9,000 people were arriving *every day* on the Greek islands, having crossed the Aegean from Turkey to Greece.[144] 1.3 million people claimed asylum in the EU in 2015.

With valid visas to fly into Europe tightly restricted, these treacherous sea voyages were the only option. People died in their thousands. The best records for the Mediterranean are held by the International Organization for Migration: at least 3,261 migrants lost their lives there in 2014, and a further 3,285 people perished in 2015. There are fewer figures available for the Aegean, but Turkish media recorded 806 deaths in 2015.[145]

For survivors, crossings were often miserable and frightening. Zoe Gardner, a migration researcher who helped new arrivals to Greece in late 2014, describes the scenes on the island of Lesvos during the worst weather: people were 'hysterical or just completely in shock or soaked through and freezing cold. It was minus six [degrees] some nights, and they had been sitting in those boats for hours.'

'On any given night you were guaranteed to have some people who were in a bad way, some people who needed medical attention,' she adds. 'You always had a *lot* of little kids,' who 'were experiencing things that adults shouldn't experience, let alone little kids.'[146]

'We have been through hell,' a passenger on another migrant boat told Bartolo.[147] So why were so many people on the move, risking everything, and what did this have to do with Britain?

## The Arab Spring, smugglers, and loads of money

The tragedies had their roots in events the previous year. By 2010, it was becoming clear that something was going seriously wrong in the region stretching from north Africa and Tunisia across to Syria in the middle east.

The Arab Spring, the name given to a series of popular uprisings against the region's despots, had stumbled. Once hailed as a democratic movement set to oust dictators, it was being crushed. In Egypt, Hosni Mubarak had been forced out of office after thirty years, thanks to mass protests led by the country's youth, but he was swiftly replaced with a shadowy military committee, followed by Islamic extremists, then more military chiefs. It was hardly what people had rallied for day after day. Libyan dictator Muammar Gaddafi lost his presidency and then his life to protesters, only for militias and religious fundamentalists to move into the vacuum and enforce their own brutal rule.

'Eighty million people were embarking on an uncharted experiment into Arab democracy, a great ball of popular hydrogen pumped to burst and rolling off a cliff,' wrote Wendell Steavenson at the onset of the uprising in Egypt.[148] The experiment, there and elsewhere, did not yield the results for which democrats had hoped.

The most horrifying news of all was coming out of Syria. Reacting to small-scale anti-government protests in 2011, Bashar Al-Assad's regime started to rain terror on its own citizens. Assad and his loyal thugs were responsible for killing hundreds of thousands of his own people and setting up a network of torture chambers for thousands more. The country descended into a civil war which still rages on.

Millions of families spilled in terror over the country's borders. Syrians who hadn't lost their freedom or loved ones had lost everything else. Between those who fled and those who were killed,

Syria lost 25% of its population in just four years.[149]

Many ended up in sprawling refugee camps in Jordan and Lebanon, or tried to rebuild their lives in Egypt or Turkey. But many Syrians looked further afield, to safety on a whole new continent. In the early years especially, the families leaving Syria were comparatively well off, certainly compared to people fleeing from north and central African countries at the same time, and could pay people to smuggle them to longer-term safety in Europe.

Suddenly, the murky international people smuggling industry had an influx of new customers. Their services were in massive demand – and as the smuggling networks expanded, so people from countries far and wide realised that if they could reach the hotspots for crossing to Europe (initially along the Libyan border, and later in Turkey) they could escape the region too. This meant eye-wateringly dangerous journeys across the desert, which by some estimates cost more lives than the sea crossings. Smuggling gangs soon charged for help navigating those deserts, too.

Smugglers' incomes went stratospheric. The journalist Patrick Kingsley, who has followed these modern smuggling routes, reckons that a single crossing from Libya to Italy on a larger wooden boat could net smugglers £180,000 in pure profit.[150] It is a multi-billion-pound business.

Once in Europe, some migrants stayed in Greece or Italy, initially in miserable government camps. But given the sheer numbers, and the pressure the Greek and Italian governments faced from their own voters not to bear the burden alone, many newcomers were discreetly waved through to other European countries. The system for deciding which European country should decide an asylum claim – known as the Dublin regulations – was breaking down, which encouraged more clandestine travel for migrants, over illegal border crossings and hiding from police and security as they headed north in their millions. Germany was a popular destination even before Angela Merkel's 2015 pledge to look after all Syrians who asked for help (the pledge was an extraordinarily brave moment of leadership and resulted in nearly 900,000 migrants arriving in Germany that year). Sweden was popular, too, as a country where many believed it would be easier to reunite with family. Both involved long, exhausting hikes through countries which didn't really want anything to do with the migrants. First Hungary and then the Balkan states erected walls along their borders. At one point Germany suspended all transport coming in from Austria, a (temporary) rejection of free movement around Europe, one of the central principles on which the EU was built.

Meanwhile, if the British government thought it could ignore the unfolding crisis it was wrong. The crisis was heading this way. The government would respond with a panicked tightening of immigration rules – but also, under pressure to show humanity amid so much suffering, with one of modern Britain's rare, proactive gestures to help refugees.

## The view from Britain

The British news covered the protests and the toppling of dictators. It also covered – maybe a little less diligently – the slow suppression of the revolutionary movement. As a foreign affairs story, the Arab Spring had the sort of ingredients the British press flocks towards: the gilded and eccentric lives of dictators, the bravery of young citizens standing up against them and the violence which followed.

Details like smuggling routes and migrant movements weren't really part of those stories, at least not at first. The press covered drownings in the Mediterranean and the Aegean, especially where the sheer number of people dying in single incidents was overwhelming, but the sense of exactly why and how people were fleeing, and where they were fleeing to, remained pretty vague. Some British journalists on the ground gave eye-witness accounts of migrants moving through north Africa and their long treks across Europe, but these articles were not front-page news (Patrick Kingsley admits to quiet frustration that his own editors at the *Guardian* relegated his earlier stories to the website rather than the paper itself, a clear sign of the priority his migration coverage initially received).[151]

It is no criticism of the media to point out that it did what it normally does and focused on the most striking tragedies and the biggest numbers. The much more complex picture, of people from myriad different countries fleeing many different problems to a range of destinations, was unfolding far beneath the radar of British opinion.

But this was soon to change. A series of images during 2015 and 2016, telling very different stories about immigration, came to define how Brits understood the crisis. They pulled public opinion and political actions in several different directions at once – and exposed all the contradictions in Britain's modern responses to immigration.

## At the gates

By late 2014 and 2015, eyes had turned to the French border. Makeshift refugee camps were springing up in Calais. More than a decade earlier, at the height of the asylum panic discussed in chapter three, the British government had agitated to get the Sangatte

refugee camp just outside Calais closed down, terrified of nightly news broadcasts showing young
men trying to break into Britain. Sangatte had been
home to just over a thousand migrants, officially, but
the new camps – swiftly named 'the jungle' – were
much bigger than that. They grew rapidly, from a
few thousand inhabitants in mid-2015 to more than
10,000 later that year.[152] This was a pitiful proportion
of the migrants who had braved untold horrors to
make it to Europe, but that isn't how it looked to
the Brits watching on, nor to a government sensi-
tive to the public mood. Ministers masterminding
the hostile environment now saw gangs of young
men barely twenty-five miles away, fenced in but
seemingly hell-bent on reaching Britain.

Videos and photos from Calais became a staple
in the news again, especially in the tabloids, which
were learning once more that migration scare stories sold papers (and now drove online traffic). In a
succession of incidents during 2015, migrants tried
to 'storm' their way onto ferries and lorries heading over the Channel (this was the word chosen by
nearly every media outlet). Accompanying videos
showed dozens of youths with their hoods up, some
with their faces covered. It looked frightening and
chaotic.[153] The British public, anxious about immigration at the best of times, watched on unhappily.

'Immigration has got an image problem,' one man would later tell a focus group. 'What I see in the media is men aged 18 to 40 coming through Calais. That is what I see.'[154]

The government duly took steps – predictably – to try and show it was toughening up against would-be migrants.

Firstly, the Immigration Minister announced that more metal fencing was being transferred to the border to stop migrants who wanted to make a final, perilous leap to Britain.[155] It may have made for a decent day's headline for the Home Office, but the idea that migrants would be put off by slightly taller fences, having braved ocean voyages by dinghy and night-time border crossings pursued by police, was laughable.

Secondly, and much more controversially, ministers broke a commitment which would have seen more young migrants taken in from Calais. The government took some kids from the French camps who had family connections in Britain, but not the number they had initially agreed, despite a high-profile campaign headed by the peer Alfred Dubs who was himself a child refugee from the Nazis.[156] (This is where public sympathy can hinder as well as help decent immigration policy: having been led to believe that the child refugees in France were toddlers and young orphans, the public was underwhelmed to find the majority were sixteen and seventeen-year-old young men, a demographic which seldom attracts much support in any situation).*

At the same time, behind the scenes, the British government joined other EU countries to enter into a whole series of deals which criss-crossed Europe and Africa. These deals are little-known and highly complex, but for ministers in Britain they had one aim: to stop migrants getting anywhere near Europe in the first place, let alone to within sight of the white cliffs of Dover. In pursuit of this goal, the British government has made some very dodgy alliances indeed. The deals made it more likely that refugees would lose their lives in pursuit of Europe. The hostile environment, once limited to British soil, was being extended into Europe and even beyond.

Britain is now helping fund something called the Khartoum Process, for example, which began life in 2014 and under which the Sudanese government has received $122 million – or about £93 million – to assist what is euphemistically called 'migration management.' In practice, the money is used to intercept would-be migrants and prevent them leaving the region. Britain wasn't a silent partner in all this: Brit-

---

* When asked about the issue in focus groups, people repeatedly said that they felt 'duped' by the promises made about child refugees in France, according to campaigners familiar with those groups. The decision by some development charities to campaign using teddy bears and empty children's beds certainly seems very unhelpful in retrospect.

ish officials have chaired the steering group behind the committee and taken what Zoe Gardner calls 'a very proactive role' in its work.[157]

'This money goes to the same regime in Khartoum whose legacy includes civil wars that eventually split the country, and who are accused of genocide in Darfur and crimes against humanity in South Kordofan and Blue Nile state,' explained specialist reporters on the news site Refugees Deeply. They continued:

> Sudan uses the so-called Rapid Support Forces (RSF) to stop refugees at the Sudan-Libya border. This paramilitary group grew out of the notorious Janjaweed, the 'devils on horseback' that committed atrocities against the civilian population in Darfur.[158]

The EU insists that none of its money goes directly to these murderous militia, but this is very murky territory indeed. 'It is extremely hard to trace where some of the EU funding goes,' according to Caitlin Chandler, a journalist who has written extensively about the region.[159]

It doesn't stop there. A different EU deal pays Libya's extremely weak government to train coastguards to pluck migrant boats out of the water long before they reach Europe. The *Financial Times* reported in 2017 that, with this money now pumping into a country with no proper government, the deal had 'sparked concerns that armed groups have in effect been contracted to stop migration and run detention centres.'[160] 'Libyan prisons are the new concentration camps,' according to Pietro Bartolo, the doctor giving medical help to people in danger of being sent back there.[161]

A little closer to the European border, yet another EU deal (this one struck in 2016) allows Greece to return all 'new irregular migrants' back to Turkey, in return for giving more cash to the Turkish government to 'manage' the refugees living there. (The deal was struck, says one senior migration expert, 'in an atmosphere of palpable panic').[162] The aim, of course, was to stop migrants crossing the Aegean, by raising the likelihood that people would be picked up from the Greek islands and sent straight back. But by swapping money for Turkish co-operation, panicking European countries handed Turkey a trump card in any future negotiation on any issue: if Turkey doesn't agree, it can simply threaten to open up the migrant routes once more. It's a dodgy deal, not a long-term fix.

Gardner is under no illusions about the outcome of these EU deals. 'Our money is going to fund detention centres where absolutely horrific human rights violations are taking place as a matter of routine,' she says. 'There's no question people are sent back to torture.'[163]

Distressingly, extending the hostile environment to Turkey, Libya and Sudan may well have had the desired effect. Violence and poverty in the region continued but the number of boats coming to Europe has slowed significantly, to their lowest level in five years.[164] When the Italian government refused to rescue migrants on board the ship *Aquarius* in 2018, leaving men, women and kids stranded off Sicily, it was a high-profile rejection of refugees at a time when fewer than ever were reaching Europe's shore.[165] It was part of a tragic pattern: as Europe retreated from helping migrant boats, including ending search and rescue missions, more people lost their lives. Over 12,000 people drowned in the three years after the Khartoum deal.[166]

Britain was complicit in turning these refugees away. But there were also signs that the country could be persuaded to reach out to people in need.

### 'That could have been my little boy'

Even while the dodgy European deals were being thrashed out, images from Calais were pushed off the news and social media. In September 2015, the migrant crisis was given a new face.

Every British newspaper, and millions of social media accounts, published pictures of tiny Alan Kurdi (originally mistakenly called Aylan in the press), a Syrian three-year-old who had drowned as his family tried to reach Greece from Turkey. Alan was still in his t-shirt and shorts, better suited to a summer family holiday. The Velcro strap on one of his shoes hung loose.

His family's boat had sunk and his body had washed up on a Turkish beach. Alan is curled-up and lifeless, face down in the surf. In other pictures, his body is being gently carried away from the sea by a policeman, cradled in the arms of a rescuer who came too late, his own face a mask of grief. They are still devastating images (see Figure 6).[167]

Figure 6. Source: International Journal of Communication

Britain's national mood was transformed by this small child. The community organising guru Matthew Bolton, a veteran of campaigns for fairer treatment of immigrants, describes how:

It was a moment that punched through the public consciousness in the most profound way, straight to the heart. It wasn't about news or politics anymore, but just about being human. I went on Al Jazeera News that evening about the UK government's response to the refugee crisis and just before going on, the make-up artist summed it up perfectly, saying: 'I never really thought about it before [the war in Syria, the refugee crisis], until I saw that photo. I've got a three-year-old. That could have been my little boy.'[168]

Syria's refugee crisis had suddenly entered Britain's front rooms and Facebook pages. Public polling around this time didn't show people completely changing their opinions on immigration, but in the week of the photos the proportion of voters who believed Britain should be a place of refuge for Syrians jumped eleven points (even if it was still a minority).[169]

There was a palpable sense that the British public, stung by the sight of death on the shores of Europe, expected more to be done to prevent future tragedies. A growing chunk of the public wanted the government to act, and act it did.

## Kneejerk liberalism

The photos were published on 2nd September. By 7th September, Prime Minister David Cameron had announced the rapid expansion of a programme to resettle Syrian refugees in Britain. The existing system had brought two hundred people to rebuild their lives here; this was increased to 20,000 people over the next five years, with refugees moved from camps on the Syrian border. As Cameron unveiled the plans, he hailed the chance to 'continue to show the world that this is a country of extraordinary compassion, always standing up for our values and helping those in need.'[170]

The process started shakily. Getting refugees to Britain was a slow process, and some councils baulked at the extra costs involved in finding homes for Syrian families.[171] But according to immigration statistics published in February 2018 – a little over two years on from Cameron's promise – more than 10,000 Syrian refugees had been settled in Britain. In crude maths, the government was halfway there, ahead of even the most optimistic official projections. Every indication was that Whitehall and local councils had found a way to work together effectively.[172]

We will look a bit more at refugee resettlement in the conclusion. But for now, we can see how a single, powerful image drew attention to a migra-

tion crisis which had otherwise been little understood. It was immediate and raw – and it forced the
government into a hurried decision to look after
more people. Some anti-immigrant voices were still
unhappy – 'opponents [of immigration] had to explain how they could be immune to the image of
dead Aylan,' grumbled Douglas Murray[173] – but that
was the point. After so many decades of kneejerk
hostility towards migrants, here was a bit of kneejerk liberalism on immigration. It could and probably should have been more people. But it was extremely welcome.

## Breaking point

On the one hand, migrants were being reduced to
faceless thugs in the press, marauding just a few
miles from the British border. On the other, government immigration policy had been forced in a
more humanitarian direction by an image of suffering which crystalized a complex picture of suffering
and loss.

None of this was taking place in a vacuum. David Cameron had made his EU referendum pledge
in January 2013, and UKIP's fortunes were on the
rise. When Cameron's Conservatives won the 2015
General Election, that referendum became inevitable. By the time migrants started gathering in Calais,

Figure 7. Source: John Gill.

and Alan Kurdi's picture was beamed across social media, campaigning for the Europe vote was well underway. Immigration was emerging as the dominant concern for people minded to vote to leave, as we have seen. A politician with the populist touch saw his chance and took it. All of which brings us onto one more image.

In June 2016, UKIP's Nigel Farage unveiled a new poster (Figure 7) urging voters to reject the EU. The Breaking Point poster had appeared in two broadsheet newspapers that morning and was now being paraded for broadcasters as well.

The poster was based on a picture taken in 2015, from the Slovenian side of its border with Croatia. It was of refugees and migrants making the long and desperate trek from the Greek coast towards Sweden and (above all) Germany, countries long idealized by refugees as a final place of safety in Europe.

The Brexiteers may not have realised it, but this snaking queue of exhausted humanity was roughly midway between Europe's border on the Greek mainland and Dover. Or to put it another way, midway between Britain and the destination which Alan Kurdi's family dreamed of but never reached.

In a campaign where immigration loomed so large, 'Breaking Point' was deeply effective. At a time when the Remain side were the ones accused of peddling fear, the poster was an incredibly simple way to summon public anxiety to the surface and none-too-gently reinforce it. It took the scenes from Calais and redramatised them for political gain, playing on several anti-immigrant ideas at once: that migrants were unruly and too numerous to predict or control; that Europe wasn't a bulwark against mass immigration but a route for immigrants to force their way to Britain; that Britain, overwhelmingly a nation of white citizens, was one European border away from being overrun by brown and black people. If the poster could be summed up in a single brutal sentence, it was this: *These people are not like us, and they are on their way here.*

For a short moment the year before, the British immigration debate had been dominated by tragedy and humanity. A small boy had died in circumstances no child should face, and briefly there was a new set of ideas about how Britain should deal with migration. We couldn't help everyone but where we *could* help we should. The government committed to lifting 20,000 Syrians out of refugee camps and bringing them to Britain, away from the bombs and the murder squads. It was a thoroughly decent and sensible gesture. At a time when the British government seemed to think about immigration mainly in terms of restrictions and clampdowns, hostility and headlines, it was a moment to be proud of.

But it didn't last. The world is a complicated place, and public and political attention moves on easily to other challenges and other ideas. By the time the official referendum campaign started in earnest, migrants were something to be scared of once again, represented by the ongoing chaos in Calais and, later, the border queues of Breaking Point. The Brexiteers exploited the fear this provoked, and they won.

Brits and immigrants had muddled through together for decades. It was seldom an easy relationship, and the majority of voters used the Brexit vote to ask for some kind of a divorce. We still don't know what that will look like and – in common with many divorces – probably no one will emerge entirely happy with the result. But one thing was clear enough. In the immigration debate, the sceptics were still winning.

# CONCLUSION
# FEELING CALLED LOVE

## Drawbridge Britain

Britain is an island. Our drawbridge was down to much of the world after the Second World War, even if we hadn't realised this meant people might actually cross it. When people started doing exactly that, the drawbridge was slowly raised. Scrambling across it was much tougher after the 60s, and so it stayed until New Labour brought it crashing back down again. Immigrants from across the world then answered the invitation to make their lives here – at which point the Brexit vote signalled a desire to see the drawbridge lifted once more.

It is worth revisiting those descriptions of public attitudes towards immigration quoted in the introduction. 'The public has not typically been enthusiastic about immigration, but they have shown a degree of pragmatism about it,' according to the experts at the British Social Attitudes Survey; Britain has 'a far-from-perfect, but nonetheless relatively easy-going, openness to the world at large,' wrote Tory peer Stephen Green.

But post-Brexit, there is a danger that Green's words in particular sound elegiac, a sepia-tinged tribute to something long gone. Is that right? Can we recover our 'openness to the world,' or is this a different Britain now, a country which has become irreversibly nervous and puckered-up about immigration and outsiders?

## Love

To try and answer that question, we must think about love.

That doesn't mean – absolutely doesn't mean – that we should be hugging each other or should spend our evenings singing around the campfire. Not *that* kind of love. But it does mean thinking more about the basic stuff on which communities are built. These are the questions which chug along beneath the surface of everyday life anyway: how do we care for our families, what will it take to stay healthy and safe, what will the future look like? Or we can boil it down to something even simpler: How can we look after the people and things we love?★

These aren't obscure ideas, they are thoroughly normal. They are the hopes and worries which underpin our lives; indeed, the same hopes and worries which underpin nearly *all* lives. Immigrants to Britain are no different: it should be no surprise to

★ This was given political form in the early 70s by one-time New Zealand Prime Minister Norman Kirk: 'All Kiwis want is someone to love, somewhere to live, somewhere to work and something to hope for.' I wrote more about this quote and its ongoing relevance in my essay for Eyewear Publishing's *Tactical Reading* in 2017.

find, in the course of this conclusion, that newcomers think mainly about the same things as everyone else. And if we are going to be optimistic about the future, that shared ground is the best place to start.

## Scepticism isn't the same as pessimism

As we have seen throughout this book, the public is sceptical about immigration. For the best part of fifty years, surveys have found that the majority of Brits want to see the number of immigrants coming into the country reduced. But as soon as we dig beneath these numbers a bit, there is much greater subtlety and nuance. The British Social Attitudes Survey found, for example, that between 2002 and 2014 people swung gradually behind the idea that immigration was good for the economy. And while the proportion of people who think immigration is bad for British culture crept upwards in those years (from 32% to 38%), Brits were still – just about – more likely to think immigration enriches our cultural life than undermines it.[174]

The public distinguishes between different *types* of immigration, too. People with skills which will boost either the economy or a treasured public service like the NHS are more welcome than unskilled immigrants; asylum seekers are pretty unpopular, but once you talk about 'genuine refugees' then you find the support of a clear majority; in some surveys, the ability to speak English is considered just as important to successful immigration and integration as a willingness to obey the law.[175]

This throws up all manner of challenges for talking about immigration, but one thing is clear. Britain today offers a mixed bag of opinions. It is not a country ravaged by anti-immigrant feeling.

All of which makes it strange that so many immigration experts act as if public opinion is much more brutal than it actually is. The think tank British Future, which is dedicated to understanding public attitudes to immigration, summed it up very neatly a few years back:

> Because everyone is talking about immigration, the dominant assumption is that the public must be deeply hostile to it. Whoever talks toughest, therefore, will be most likely to connect with them. This argument comes not only from migration sceptics who claim to own public opinion and 'speak for ordinary people'; it is also accepted by migration liberals who concede public opinion to those who are opposed to immigration. Our research shows that this is not where the public is on immigration. The assumption of public hostility is a mistaken one.[176]

In other words, pro- and anti-immigration folk alike assume that the public rejects immigration outright. Yet this isn't true. The public does not reject immigration out of hand. People are unpredictable and their opinions are far, far more complex than we sometimes allow.

## Who thinks what

British Future, along with charities like Hope Not Hate, make a compelling case for separating British attitudes on immigration roughly into three. A quarter of people at one end are staunchly pro-immigration and believe it brings lots of cultural and economic benefits to the country (a small slice of these would get rid of borders completely); a quarter of people at the other are deeply unhappy about immigration and see its impact as very negative (including a 'small, significant and worrying minority [who] may hold quite toxic, racist views'). Bigger than both by far is the chunk of the population in the centre, around half the British population, whom the think tank calls the 'moderate middle' (in the preface we called them the 'sceptical middle'). This covers a range of opinions, from people who broadly welcome immigration but think change is happening too fast to people who are concerned about immigration but can see the benefits when it is managed effectively.[177]

At the margins, we find views that are either socially unacceptable (racism) or politically implausible (a complete end to all international borders). It is the vast spread of people in between, the ones with moderate opinions, who are crucial. People are nowhere near as hostile as we have come to suppose. Which leads us to a much more fruitful question for thinking about the future, and one with which we will conclude this book. If there is common ground on immigration after all, how do we find it together?

What follows are a few home-spun but hopefully helpful ideas for where the immigration debate can go next, a grab-bag of suggestions to kick-start the next set of conversations. If not a migration cap (which has failed year after year after year) and not a hostile environment (which doesn't work morally or practically) then what?

The next few pages look first at the language we use and then at the policies governments could pursue. If this book and its conclusions has borrowed ideas from the across the spectrum, from activists to academics to Labour voters in working-class towns to UKIP spokespeople, don't be too surprised. That moderate middle is very wide and can take us all the way from left-wing campaigners on one side to the architects of Brexit on the other. The immigration debate is there to be won.

## Language is important

*Sloganeering*
People who campaign against immigration are very good at it. People who campaign on the benefits of immigration are not. This is blunt, but unless we accept this fact then we will never change it.

Here, for example, is Douglas Murray in the opening pages of his book *The Strange Death of Europe*. He thinks immigration is bad for the country, and here he is writing about post-war migration:

> Soon Europe got hooked on migration and could not stop the flow if it wanted to. The result was that what had been Europe – the home of the European peoples – gradually became a home for the entire world. [178]

Murray's book is quite odd (at one point it calls on the British government to pursue policies which will encourage its citizens to have more sex), but he is a wonderful writer. Whatever one makes of its argument, *The Strange Death of Europe* is full of deft short sentences like these. In barely forty words, Murray has compared immigration to an addiction over which Europe has lost control and linked this to a profound territorial and cultural loss. The whole concept of 'home' is brought into question. Murray also chooses the word 'flow' for the movement of migrants: *The Strange Death of Europe* is inflammatory in places but he is far too smart to advertise this by dropping into the cruder, Powell-ite language of, say, 'invasions' or 'swarms'.

That trope of losing control, subtly introduced here, was central to the Brexit campaign of course. The Leavers, too, offered some perfectly pitched campaigning. 'Take back control' was a short, vague and alluring phrase, ideal for political rhetoric. It meant taking back control over British borders and stemming Murray's 'flow' of immigrants – or indeed, taking back control of British laws from European courts, or of our businesses from interfering Brussels bureaucrats. Whatever potential voters were worried about, 'take back control' offered an appealing alternative.

Anti-immigration voices are good at this stuff. Think of the headlines they have generated: 'Immigration backlog is the size of Iceland' (*The Telegraph*, 2012); 'UK 'would need a new city the size of Birmingham every two years for migrants' if we go for 'soft' Brexit' (*The Sun*, 2017); 'One per cent of entire Slovakian population living in Britain' (*The Telegraph*, 2011). We can see the pattern here. Anti-immigration campaigners are generally very good at finding concise and memorable ways to get their point across.

And the other side? Their slogans are awful.

One slogan popular with pro-immigration campaigners – 'No one is illegal' – is about as hopeless as it gets (see Figure 8).[179] Public concern about illegal immigration is extremely high, and certainly much higher than for people who live in Britain legally. The slogan bucks the cardinal rule of campaigning, by adopting the language of the other side. Certainly, it will be harder to persuade people to support a pro-immigration campaign if you are using precisely the word – 'illegal' – which makes them worried in the first place.

Figure 8. Source: Tim & Selena Middleton

The same might be said of 'Borders kill,' a phrase seen on far too many placards at campaign rallies. This may well literally be true – history is full of people losing their lives in their desperate attempts to evade border controls – but it too breaks a pretty basic rule of modern campaigning. Even people sympathetic to your cause won't enjoy being told they had better agree with you or they are murderers. Very few normal punters will nod their head and sign up to your cause. It may even harden their own scepticism or, most likely, they will filter it out and get on with their lives entirely untouched by what they have heard.

## Authenticity

Language matters, and so does the general tone that surrounds it. This brings greater cause for optimism. Authenticity is everything.

We can look to the US to see this play out. In June 2014, the US Republican Party was in civil war. Tea Party activists from the Republican right-wing were trying to topple two sitting politicians from their own party, Senator Lindsey Graham and Congressman Eric Cantor.

Mark Thompson tells the story in his excellent book *Enough Said*. In both cases, the Tea Party candidates argued that they would be tougher on immigration than the incumbent. It was generally felt that Cantor, who had considered some progressive immigration reforms but was relatively hard-line on the issue, would emerge unscathed. Graham, though, was presumed to be in real trouble. He had been an 'outspoken advocate' of progressive reform for years – far too nice to immigrants for the Tea Party's liking.

In the end, the pundits' wisdom was wholly wrong. Graham won and Cantor lost. Amid all the variables, one explanation lies in immigration. Graham may not have held the views (or the voting record) that people liked, but he had something else: authenticity.

Thompson quotes Graham after his victory, trying to explain why he prevailed and Cantor did not:

> You've got to take a firm stance one way or the other. ... The worst thing you can do on an issue like this is to be hard to figure out. And I am not hard to figure out on immigration.

Thompson argues persuasively that Graham, through the consistency of his support for immigration reform, won 'the grudging respect even of voters who take a different view.' There was no such luck for Cantor who sent mixed signals, sometimes sympathetic towards migrants to the US and sometimes turning against them. It just wasn't clear what he stood for – and he lost.[180]

Closer to home, this was a problem which dogged Ed Miliband as Labour leader after 2010. Miliband was a metropolitan policy-wonk who was comfortable with immigration, yet was presented by his spin-doctors as an everyday guy who shared the worries of Labour's core voters. It wasn't authentic, and the public could sense that a mile off. And it is the same problem now which confronts the Liberal Democrats: do they stay the course as a confident party of free movement in Europe or push tougher lines on immigration which are less authentically liberal but would, in theory, chime with the public mood?

### Don't insult people

Finally on language: when we talk about immigration, we talk about people's lives. Let's not insult anyone when we do. This should be obvious but somehow it is not.

To take one popular theory heard pretty regularly from commentators and business leaders, and certainly down the pub: immigrants are willing to do the jobs that native Brits won't.

In his excellent book on political communication, *Words That Work*, the American pollster Frank Luntz returns to the same argument over and over again. 'It's not what you say,' he insists, 'it's what people hear.'[181] In other words, don't think about communication as a thing you *do*, think about it as something another person experiences and interprets and responds to. So in our example, what do British people hear when told that immigrants are stepping in to fill jobs that they won't do?

Here is a man called Adrian Dixon, who worked on farms in Boston in Lancashire for twenty years before becoming a taxi driver, quoted in Emily Dugan's *Finding Home*:

> When I was a farm labourer the wages were £300 a week. They're worse now. [...] this is about farmers knowing they can pay less. It used to be if you were a farmhand round here you were made up. Yes, it was hard graft but you were paid fairly and it'd be you that had money to buy drinks in the pub and get a house.[182]

And here is Gawain Towler, UKIP's former head spin doctor:

> To hear *Oh, migrants are better workers than Britons*, it really hacks me off. How dare they? [...] It pisses on the poor, the working class, the British poor, the ones we are supposed to care about, the ones that politicians are paid to care about.[183]

This is an area where getting the language and tone right is especially important. There are 2.2 million EU workers in Britain, according to experts in parliament,[184] and it is the country's lowest-paid workers, Brits and immigrants alike, who can sometimes see their wages squeezed when the country welcomes in more migrants. Different studies have found different results: the Oxford Migration Observatory quotes a study from 2006 which says that 'in the unskilled and semi-skilled service sector, a 1% rise in the share of migrants [in the country] reduced average wages in that occupation by nearly 0.5%'. A later study found a reduction of 0.2%.[185] A still later piece of research from the London School of Economics, conducted after the economic crash of 2008, found no link between falling wages for low-skilled labour and higher immigration, and laid the blame instead squarely on the recession.[186]

The truth was that people could either blame bosses who chose to dish-out rubbish pay or the immigrants who were being exploited by the same bosses. If the argument blaming immigrants has been more compelling, it is worth trying to work out why. Dixon and Towler are both talking about life at the hardest end of the economy, and are doing so by evoking the basics of pride and respect. Their points of reference are the stuff of real life: the dignity involved in knowing you can save for the future and have enough left to stand your round after a day's work. This is a compelling narrative: a generation of young people have been frozen out of fair jobs and pay by a grim coalition of greedy bosses, immigrants who will accept lower pay, and a political establishment which couldn't care less. The sense of community and loss here is palpable, and compares with the cold, transactional language of the old pro-immigration trope which simply says that one person can step into a job when another person leaves it. Both accounts are true, and there is no doubt that people who like immigration also love their communities – but Dixon and Towler have a much finer feel for communicating what is being lost along the way. It is hardly a surprise that the more personal and more compelling argument makes greater headway, but it also provokes the question: when will we get an effective, well-communicated critique not of immigrants but of big business, and the social impact of companies which have done extremely well out of immigration but under-paid and under-valued once thriving communities while they did so?

## Policy: what works

Tony Blair had many mantras in government, some more memorable than others. One of the more obscure ones may also have been the most important: 'What matters is what works.'

As with most Blair mantras it needs a bit of unpicking, but one rough translation would be: *Ordinary people care more about things being done right than the ideology which underlies it, so let's follow the evidence of what actually works.* He had a point, one which can be applied to immigration as well as other areas of policy.

*Refugee resettlement in the 90s*

We looked at one resettlement programme in chapter five, and the moment of kneejerk liberalism which will end up rehoming 20,000 Syrian refugees in this country by 2020. There is plenty of evidence that this programme is already pretty successful – and evidence, too, that Britain has transformed thousands of lives this way in the past.

In 1998, for example, Kosovan Albanians (or Kosovars)* were facing massacre in the Balkans, terrorised by Slobodan Miloševiç's Serbian forces in a corner of eastern Europe becoming synonymous with conflict.

The west was slow to react but assembled awesome force when it did. A two-month bombing offensive by NATO in March 1999 received hawkish

---

* In the Balkans, even the choice of words for describing nationalities is complex and controversial. I have followed the example of Tim Judah in calling Kosovan Albanians 'Kosovars', as he does in his excellent book on the conflict.

backing from Blair's government. As the dust settled on a decade of conflict, it became clear that the international community also had big decisions to make about refugees from the war.

Families had been forced over the Macedonian border into miserable, makeshift camps, where they were now stuck. The UN called for emergency resettlement of Kosovar families out of these camps, including to Britain. The British agreed to accept 4,346 Kosovar refugees under the UN scheme, who started to arrive in April 1999.[187] There is a telling note in the diaries kept at the time by Blair's chief spin doctor, Alastair Campbell. 'We could deal with the humanitarian crisis but we had to be able to show military success,' Campbell wrote: 'the two strategies had to work in tandem.' [188] Britain could lead in both military might and humanitarian responsibility, he implied, a message gratefully received by thousands of Kosovars but tragically not applied in later New Labour conflicts, when survivors from the carnage in Iraq received no such offer.

The government could have done much, much more to resettle Kosovar families – Germany gave shelter to three times as many families under the same programme – but welcoming in thousands of refugees set in motion other developments.

At the same time that Kosovars were being flown direct from the Macedonian border to their new homes in Britain, more than ten thousand of their countrymen and women were in the country in limbo, waiting for a decision on asylum applications. The future for these asylum seekers was extremely uncertain, and in the meantime they received almost no financial and social support.

Within months the government, confronted with growing evidence of how differently these two groups of Kosovars were being treated, gave in to the inevitable. In June, Home Secretary Jack Straw agreed to let the 11,000 or so asylum seekers who had arrived before the start of NATO bombing stay in Britain, on more generous terms if not quite the same as those enjoyed by their resettled compatriots.[189]

One moment of decency towards vulnerable people had been followed by another. We can pick holes in these sorts of resettlement policies: schemes could always be bigger, or last longer, or applied to more countries. It would help if ministers made the decisions more quickly, and worked more closely with local councils who would end up hosting the refugees. But legitimate criticisms of schemes shouldn't mask a bigger point. Occasionally, Britain is capable of delivering the humanitarian response that a moment demands. Resettlement works, but it remains rare. We should do more of it.

*Integration (or: immigrants are normal)*

Integration, as defined in the preface, is essentially a deal between Brits and immigrants. The British are welcoming but want to see newcomers sign up to a few basics: commitment to English and the rule of law, and a readiness to contribute to society. This is perfectly achievable even if it isn't always easy, but anti-immigrant voices will tell us that this is either impossible or not worth the effort. Recall the Breaking Point poster: it played on the fear that immigrants are an indistinguishable mass, incompatible with Britain and its values.

Here is a new way to approach the whole question (and this is where the love comes in). Immigrants aren't alien or odd or unusual. They are overwhelmingly ordinary.

How do we know? Because they keep telling us. In 2018 some Poles in Britain set up their own party, Duma Polska (which translates as Polish Pride), which put up a hundred candidates in the spring's local elections. So did they offer a narrow appeal to nationalist voters? Not a bit of it. Duma Polska wanted to raise concerns about xenophobia in the aftermath of Brexit, but beyond that their concerns were the normal hodge-podge of local issues and idealism one associates with smaller political parties. As Duma Polska's founder told one London newspaper:

> We are here to represent everybody who is tired of Westminster politics. Locally, we want safer streets and proper refuse collections. We want to build a million homes and plant a million trees. And we want to abolish council tax, which is unfair and regressive.[190]

Not special treatment for one group of people but better bin collection. It is all very, well, British.

Or for an older example, the concerns for the Somali community in Cardiff – one of the best established in Britain, since the docks opened the city to the world early in the twentieth century – resemble the concerns carried by any other community. Asked back in 2009 what most worried young British-Somalis, the Somali Advice Centre reeled off a list including jobs for young people and the prohibitive cost of buying your own home. This isn't to say that Somalis in Britain haven't faced a tough time over the years, but that their fundamental interests are predictable. They are the same nuts and bolts of social life that we all seek.*

And let's revisit those refugees for a moment.

Here is the story of Ahsanullah Ahsas, a 'shy, gaunt' Afghan child who, having seen his father shot dead in front of him by the Taliban, was smug-

---

* I visited the Somali Advice Centre during work for the local MP in summer 2009. I went in with the (forgivable) expectation that they would want to talk about racial discrimination and was pleasantly relieved to find their worries were far more mundane.

gled into Britain and was helped by charities to start rebuilding his life. This is the *Guardian* again:

> This young man [...] is making plans. Granted his refugee status, he says he feels a sense of belonging in Leeds. 'When I was small, I wanted to be a nurse,' he says. 'I need to find my family, continue my education, with part-time work, and quickly learn English, then I would like to study nursing. And learn to drive. I want to play some sport, too. Then life will be good.' [191]

This is the pleasant but rather dull truth about immigrants. Their values are the same as everybody else's. Refugee kids – the very people who we might think have experienced things so alien to the rest of us – crave a sense of belonging, a good family life, a job, the chance to run around a sports field, the freedom of a car to drive. It is the same stuff as everyone else, in all its seriousness and silliness. And you don't always get what you want, of course, a discovery that young refugees will make as they grow up in the same way as everyone else.

Good politicians know it too. To look across the Atlantic one last time, this is from a 2017 *Prospect* profile of Steve Bullock, the popular Governor of Montana. Bullock is a successful Democrat in a state which also voted heavily for Donald Trump. *Prospect* quotes him:

> If there is overlap, it's making people know that I will fight for them, and that I work for them. I'm not sure that the values are that different in Manhattan, Montana; Manhattan, Kansas; or Manhattan, New York. People want to feel safe, have good schools, and want their kids to do better than they did. [192]

Safety, a better education, a stronger future for the people we love. This is what we all value. It isn't rocket science.

Other writers have reached a variety of different conclusions on this question. Paul Collier, whose book *Exodus* warns at length about the difficulty of any meaningful integration once an immigrant community reaches a certain size, is doubtful that this common ground would make much difference.[193] On the contrary, Kate Fox, the anthropologist, has argued that immigrants to Britain 'quite consciously, deliberately, cleverly and even mockingly pick and choose among the behaviours and customs of their host culture,' and do so fairly quickly on arriving. [194] Both would argue that facts and social science back them up. Surely we can at least start by listening to what immigrants themselves are telling us – and they have told us over and over again that their essential concerns and worries and values are no different from our own.

*Integration in practice*

So what can local governments, or national officials or members of the public, do to help this along? UKIP's Towler has a suggestion. Once a Conservative candidate for one of the poorest areas of Scotland, Towler saw up-close the resentment that festers when there is no appeal to common values.

In the early 1990s, half a dozen Bosnian families came to live in council schemes in Glasgow's Merryhill estate. Flats in schemes which had been neglected by the local council for years, he says, were suddenly being improved and new goods moved in. But these flats were going to the migrants, not longer-term residents. (Intriguingly, the lessons learned by those Leicester campaigners who secured private housing for Ugandan Asian refugees in the 70s weren't applied by the government twenty years later).

Towler is sure that, had the frustrated residents known more about their new neighbours, tensions would have been far lower:

> If the local council had merely bothered to tell the people on the estate what was going on, the welcome would have been significant. But they didn't bother to tell them, they just spent all this dosh, rammed

them into these estates without explaining to their next-door neighbours why they were here. Because if you'd actually told them, you know what, there would have been no trouble at all. Because people are decent really. Most people, most of the time, are decent.

He adds:

I'd have got the council to spend five hundred quid, welcoming all the new people in, to invite them, *Tell your story*. And if you can't tell your story, we [the council] will tell your story for you, so that your community, the community you have just moved into, know why you are here, and know why they [the council] are right to look after you.[195]

It isn't quite that simple, of course. No experts on trauma would encourage the idea that vulnerable migrants should feel under pressure to make public their experiences even if it was through a council official. But in some ways, these are the details which get ironed into shape. The intent is the more important thing. As Towler says, 'most people, most of the time, are decent.' He is right. And the growth of community sponsorship programmes today – where neighbourhoods come together to prepare for, and welcome, newly-arriving immigrants to Britain – is a big step in the right direction. Governments have all too often made a mess of integration policy, so there is room for the public to do more and do it better.

## And finally: becoming British

Immigration is a funny old thing. At its most essential, it refers to nothing more than where in the world someone lives, a very simple concept indeed. But the question of who gets to live in Britain – and how they should behave when they get here – has emerged as one of the most controversial issues of the modern age. Immigration has changed the lives of millions of people, affecting not just those on the move but those already here. It has sparked arguments and sold newspapers. It has helped win, and lose, elections.

And with it comes the question of integration, and how people can live alongside one another, our cultures intact but not so distinct that we end up living separate lives. That fusing of cultures means that immigration has changed Britain but also that millions of immigrants have gradually become more British.

Well, what does *that* mean? Recent political attempts to define and enforce Britishness have failed, maybe inevitably given that one entrenched bit of the British character is not to take such definitions seriously.

But researchers recently hit on an innovative way to think about immigration. They took a sideways glance at opinion polling and found that the longer an immigrant had lived in Britain, the more sceptical they became about immigration as a whole. Even a substantial minority of new migrants – a third of those who had been here under five years – thought immigration levels to Britain were too high. This rose to well over half of immigrants who had lived here for longer.[196]

Or to put this another way, as immigrants integrate into society so they adopt that most British trait: they grow wary of more immigration. They join the ranks of sceptics who muddle along in their communities. It is bizarre yet heart-warming. A new generation of pragmatic, cynical and utterly normal Brits is emerging in front of our eyes.

# NOTES

1 C. Cook, 'Why do England's high-rises keep failing fire tests?', BBC, 29 June 2017 http://www.bbc.co.uk/news/uk-40418266

2 K. Bennhold, 'On London's streets, black cabs and uber fight for a future', *New York Times*, 4th July 2017 https://www.nytimes.com/2017/07/04/world/europe/london-uk-brexit-uber-taxi.html

3 The ITV story can be seen at 'Grenfell: Less than 15% of donations have reached survivors', 11th August 2017 http://www.itv.com/news/2017-08-11/grenfell-less-than-15-of-donations-have-reached-survivors/

4 G. Philo, E. Briant and P. Donald, *Bad News for Refugees*, Pluto Press, 2013, p. 8.

5 See the House of Commons Library research briefing into immigration detention in the UK, June 13th 2017 http://researchbriefings.parliament.uk/ResearchBriefing/Summary/CBP-7294

6 In *Inquiry into asylum support for children and young people*, September 2013, p. 23. https://www.childrenssociety.org.uk/sites/default/files/tcs/asylum_support_inquiry_report_final.pdf

7 See *Transatlantic Trends: Mobility, migration, and integration*, September 2014, Chart 3 http://www.gmfus.org/publications/transatlantic-trends-mobility-migration-and-integration

8 See C. Vargas-Silva, *The Fiscal Impact of Immigration in the UK*, 30th May 2017 http://www.migrationobservatory.ox.ac.uk/resources/briefings/the-fiscal-impact-of-immigration-in-the-uk/; H. Warrell, 'EU migrants pay £20bn more in taxes than they receive', *Financial Times*, November 4th 2014 https://www.ft.com/content/c49043a8-6447-11e4-b219-00144feabdc0; Neil Reeder, *Neighbourhood Economic Models*, August 2017 https://www.powertochange.org.uk/wp-content/uploads/2017/11/Neighbourhood-Economic-Models.pdf; Office for National Statistics, 'Personal well-being in the UK: October 2016 to September 2017', 26th February 2018 https://www.ons.gov.uk/peoplepopulationandcommunity/wellbeing/bulletins/measuringnationalwellbeing/october2016toseptember2017

9 S. Blinder and W. Allen, 'Briefing: UK Public Opinion Towards Immigration: Overall Attitudes and Level of Concern', 28th November 2016, Figure 3 http://www.migrationobservatory.ox.ac.uk/resources/briefings/uk-public-opinion-toward-immigration-overall-attitudes-and-level-of-concern/

10 British Future, *How to Talk About Immigration*, 2014, p. 54 https://www.britishfuture.org/wp-content/uploads/2014/11/How-To-Talk-About-Immigration-FINAL.pdf

11 R. Ford and K. Lymperopoulou, 'Immigration: How attitudes in the UK compare with Europe' in British Social Attitudes 34, August 2017, p. 3. http://bsa.natcen. ac.uk/media/39148/bsa34_immigration_final.pdf

12 S. Green, *Brexit and the British: Who Are We Now?*, Haus Publishing, 2017, pp. 17-18.

13 E. Dugan, *Finding Home: Real Stories of Migrant Britain*, Icon Books, 2016, p. 3.

14 Interview with Pauline Bock, 23rd November 2017. All quotes from this interview unless otherwise stated.

15 See http://www.britishelectionstudy.com/bes-findings/what-mattered-most-to-you-when-deciding-how-to-vote-in-the-eu-referendum/#.WqZsLejwY2w

16 N. Cecil, 'Minister Priti Patel: Quit EU to Save our Curry Houses', *Evening Standard*, 18th May 2016 https://www.standard.co.uk/news/politics/minister-priti-patel-quit-eu-to-save-our-curry-houses-a3251071.html

17 The 5,000-13,000 estimate, made for the Home Office by academics at Kings College London, can be accessed at http://www.ucl.ac.uk/~uctpb21/reports/HomeOffice25_03.pdf

18 See the House of Commons Library research briefing into migration statistics, February 2018, Table 5 http://researchbriefings.parliament.uk/ResearchBriefing/Summary/SN06077

19 Blinder and Allen, 'Briefing: UK Public Opinion Towards Immigration'.

20 J. Elgot, 'Liam Fox: EU Nationals in UK One of Main Cards in Brexit Negotiations', *The Guardian*, 4th October 2016 https://www.theguardian.com/politics/2016/oct/04/liam-fox-refuses-to-guarantee-right-of-eu-citizens-to-remain-in-uk

21 M. Busby, 'EU Nationals Deportation Letters an 'Unfortunate Error' says May', *The Guardian*, 23rd August 2017 https://www.theguardian.com/politics/2017/aug/23/home-office-apologises-for-letters-threatening-to-deport-eu-nationals

22 P. Bock, 'A Year In My Life As a Brexit Bargaining Chip', *New Statesman*, 23rd June 2017 https://www.newstatesman.com/politics/brexit/2017/03/brexit-bargaining-chip-eu-citizens-year-life

23 The full letter can be read at https://www.facebook.com/notes/theresa-may/i-know-our-country-would-be-poorer-if-you-left-and-i-want-you-to-stay/1989705411046222/

24 Office for National Statistics, 'Migration Since the Brexit Vote: What's Changed in Six Charts', 30th November 2017 https://www.ons.gov.uk/peoplepopulationand-community/populationandmigration/internationalmigration/articles/migrationsin-cethebrexitvotewhatschangedinsixcharts/2017-11-30

25 Graph from https://www.migrationwatchuk.org/statistics-net-migration-statistics

26 D. Murray, *The Strange Death of Europe: Immigration, Identity, Islam*, Bloomsbury, 2017, p. 31.

27 A transcript of Michael Howard's speech can be accessed from http://news.bbc.co.uk/1/hi/uk_politics/vote_2005/frontpage/4430453.stm

28 Philo, Briant and Donald, *Bad News For Refugees*, p. 50.

29 Robert Winder, *Bloody Foreigners: The Story of Immigration to Britain*, Brown, 2004, p. 338.

30 See J. Allen and A. Parnes, *Shattered: Inside Hillary Clinton's Doomed Campaign*, Crown Book, 2017, 246.

31 M. Nowack and B. Branford, 'France Elections: What Makes Marie Le Pen Far Right?', BBC, 10th February 2017 http://www.bbc.co.uk/news/world-europe-38321401

32 C. Kroet, 'Viktor Orbán: Migrants Are a Poison', Politico, 27th July 2016 https://www.politico.eu/article/viktor-orban-migrants-are-a-poison-hungarian-prime-minister-europe-refugee-crisis/

33 Interview with Heather Staff, 11th March 2018.

34 J. Henley, 'Angela Merkel Wins Fourth Term But AfD Make Gains', *The Guardian*, 24th September 2017 https://www.theguardian.com/world/live/2017/sep/24/german-elections-2017-angela-merkel-cdu-spd-afd-live-updates

35 D. Charter, 'Far-Right Freedom Party Will Control Austrian Army In Coalition Deal', *Times*, 18th December 2017 https://www.thetimes.co.uk/article/far-right-freedom-party-will-control-austrian-army-in-coalition-deal-00hdlmf8p

36 T. Embury-Dennis, 'Italy's Deputy PM Salvini Called For 'Mass Cleansing, Street by Street, Quarter by Quarter,' Newly Released Footage Reveals', *The Independent*, 21st June 2018 https://www.independent.co.uk/news/world/europe/italy-matteo-salvini-video-immigration-mass-cleansing-roma-travellers-far-right-league-party-a8409506.html

37 D. Alexander, 'How Donald Trump Shifted Kids-Cancer Charity Money Into His Business', *Forbes*, June 29th 2017 https://www.forbes.com/sites/danalexander/2017/06/06/how-donald-trump-shifted-kids-cancer-charity-money-into-his-business/#4bbba91e6b4a

38 M. Haberman, G. Thrush and P. Baker, 'Inside Trump's Hour-by-Hour Battle For Self-Preservation', *New York Times*, 9th December 2017 https://www.nytimes.com/2017/12/09/us/politics/donald-trump-president.html

39 The full Michael Give interview on 3rd June 2016 can be accessed at https://www.youtube.com/watch?v=GGgiGtJk7MA

40 R. Littlejohn, 'Those Wicked 'Tory cuts' – Women and Children First', *Daily Mail*, 15th February 2011 http://www.dailymail.co.uk/debate/article-1357039/Tory-cuts-Women-children-first.html

41 See http://www.pressgazette.co.uk/sun-accused-of-swan-bake-myth-making/

42 R. Shepherd, *Enoch Powell: A Biography,* Random House, 1996, pp. 7, 18, 40, 90, 116.

43 See D. Sandbrook, *Never Had It So Good: A History of Britain From Suez to The Beatles*, Abacus, 2005, p. 311; R. Cavendish, 'Arrival of SS Empire Windrush' in *History Today*, June 1998 https://www.historytoday.com/richard-cavendish/arrival-ss-empire-windrush

44 Sandbrook, *Never Had It So Good*, p. 312.

45 D. Olusoga, *Black and British: A Forgotten History*, MacMillan, 2016, p. 498.

46 See M. Rendall and J. Salt, 'The foreign-born population' in *Focus On People and Migration*, Palgrave, 2005, p. 134.

47 Olusoga, *Black and British*, p. 493.

48 Sandbrook, *Never Had It So Good*, p. 329.

49 *Ibid.*

50 Olusoga, *Black and British*, p. 511.

51 Sheppard, *Enoch Powell*, p. 72.

52 Sandbrook, *Never Had It So Good*, p. 313.

53 Olusoga, *Black and British*, p. 499.

54 W. James, 'The black experience in twentieth-century Britain' in P. Morgan and S. Hawkins (eds), *Black Experience and the Empire*, Oxford University Press, 2006, p. 371.

55 R. Sheppard, *Enoch Powell*, p. 133.

56 The text of the *Telegraph* article is accessible at http://www.enochpowell.net/fr-82.html

57 See Winder, *Bloody Foreigners*, pp. 279-281.

58 The full text of the Rivers of Blood speech can be accessed at https://www.telegraph.co.uk/comment/3643823/Enoch-Powells-Rivers-of-Blood-speech.html

59 S. Heffer, *Like the Roman: The Life of Enoch Powell*, Faber, 2014, p. 451.

60 Sheppard, *Enoch Powell*, pp. 340, 363.

61 Ibid., p. 393.

62 Ibid., p. 330.

63 Ibid., p. 481.

64 Ibid., pp. 355-356.

65 Heffer, *Like the Roman*, p. 454.

66 M. Collins, 'Immigration and Opinion Polls in Postwar Britain' in *Modern History Review*, 2016, pp. 8-13.

67 Olusoga, *Black and British*, p. xi.

68 Winder, *Bloody Foreigners*, pp. 300-301.

69 Private interview, January 2018.

70 Quoted in D. Sandbrook, *State of Emergency: The Way We Were, Britain 1970-74*, Allen Lane, 2010, p. 270.

71 See 'Le Pen and Britain', *The Guardian*, 24th April 2002 https://www.theguardian.com/politics/2002/apr/24/thefarright.france

72 See M. Walker, *The National Front*, Fontana, 1977.

73 Rendall and Salt, 'The Foreign Born Population', p. 133.

74 Quoted in BBC, '1971: UK Restricts Commonwealth Migrants' http://news.bbc.co.uk/onthisday/hi/dates/stories/february/24/newsid_2518000/2518513.stm

75 Andy McSmith, *No Such Thing as Society: A History of Britain in the 1980s*, Constable, 2011, p. 14.

76 Ibid., p. 30.

77 Ibid., p. 89.

78 Sandbrook, *State of Emergency*, p. 267.

79 Quoted in A. Travis, 'Ministers Hunted For Island to House Asians', *The Guardian*, 1st January 2003 https://www.theguardian.com/uk/2003/jan/01/past.politics; Sandbrook, *State of Emergency*, p. 255.

80 Sandbrook, *State of Emergency*, pp. 256-257.

81 The BBC reproduced the advert on the fortieth anniversary of the first Ugandan Asian refugees arriving in Leicester, which can be viewed at https://www.bbc.co.uk/news/uk-england-leicestershire-19165216

82 Ibid., pp. 257-259.

83 H. Qureshi, 'Passport, visa, virginity? A mother's tale of immigration in the 1970s', *The Guardian*, 13th May 2011 https://www.theguardian.com/lifeandstyle/2011/may/13/virginity-tests-uk-immigrants-1970s

84 Ibid.

85 Ibid. See also A. Travis, 'Virginity Tests for Immigrants 'Reflected Dark Age Prejudices' of 1970s Britain', *The Guardian*, 8th May 2011 https://www.theguardian.com/uk/2011/may/08/virginity-tests-immigrants-prejudices-britain

86 An excerpt from the interview can be accessed at https://www.youtube.com/watch?v=sHhKI5ijnxQ&t=189s. A full transcript is published at https://www.margaretthatcher.org/document/103485

87 McSmith, *No Such Thing as Society*, p. 87.

88 Winder, *Bloody Foreigners*, p. 292.

89 Ibid., p. 308.

90 E. Consterdine, 'How New Labour Made Britain Into a Migration State', *The Conversation*, 1st December 2017 https://theconversation.com/how-new-labour-made-britain-into-a-migration-state-85472

91 See T. Finch and D. Goodhart (eds.), *Immigration Under Labour*, Prospect/IPPR, 2010, pp. 3, 19-21.

92 A. Neather, 'Don't Listen to the Whingers – London Needs Immigrants', *Evening Standard*, 23rd October 2009 https://www.standard.co.uk/news/dont-listen-to-the-whingers-london-needs-immigrants-6786170.html

93 Finch and Goodhart, *Immigration Under Labour*, p. 6.

94 See https://www.gov.uk/government/publications/fairer-faster-and-firmer-a-modern-approach-to-immigration-and-asylum

95 C. McGreal, 'War in Congo Kills 45,000 Each Month', *The Guardian*, 23rd January 2008  https://www.theguardian.com/world/2008/jan/23/congo.international

96 Unsigned article, 'Campaigners claim asylum seeker is beaten on Congo return', *Evening Gazette*, 8th June 2009 https://www.gazettelive.co.uk/news/local-news/campaigners-claim-asylum-seeker-beaten-3717709

97 C. Ramos, 'Congo is torturing citizens who have been refused asylum in the UK', *The Guardian*, 16th January 2012 https://www.theguardian.com/commentisfree/libertycentral/2012/jan/16/congo-torture-refused-asylum-uk

98 C. Karumba, 'Rape Capital of the World', *New Statesman*, 2nd July 2010 https://www.newstatesman.com/blogs/the-staggers/2010/07/congo-drc-women-war-violence

99 D. Gadher, 'Britain rejects rape victims' asylum pleas', *Sunday Times*, 3rd November 2013 https://www.thetimes.co.uk/article/britain-rejects-rape-victims-asylum-pleas-vqwf5slxlr9

100 F. Bawdon, ''Why aren't sexual abuse reforms being applied to asylum seekers?', *The Guardian*, 8th March 2013 https://www.theguardian.com/law/2013/mar/08/sexual-abuse-asylum-seekers

101 All data from S. Blinder, *Migration to the UK: Asylum*, 26th October 2017 http://www.migrationobservatory.ox.ac.uk/resources/briefings/migration-to-the-uk-asylum/

102 D. Miliband, *Rescue: Refugees and the Political Crisis of Our Time*, Ted Books, 2017, p. 37.

103 In Finch and Goodhart, *Immigration Under Labour*, p. 17.

104 Winder, *Bloody Foreigners*, p. 329.

105 O. King, *House Music: The Oona King Diaries*, Bloomsbury, 2007, p. 117.

106 J. Allsopp, A. Burridge, M. Griffiths, N. Gill and R. Rotter, 'Inside Britain's Asylum Appeal System – What It's Like to Challenge the Home Office', *The Conversation*, 18th December 2017 https://theconversation.com/inside-britains-asylum-appeal-system-what-its-like-to-challenge-the-home-office-88907

107 D. Newling, 'Migration Officer 'Sang Um Bongo Song to an Asylum Seeker from Congo'', *Daily Mail*, 4th March 2010 http://www.dailymail.co.uk/news/article-1255066/UK-Border-Agency-whistleblower-alleges-staff-racially-prejudiced-asylum-seekers.html

108 Unsigned article, ''I Couldn't Sleep at Night. Had I Sent Them Home to their Deaths?' As ex Asylum Official Tells All', BBC, 13th January 2017 http://www.bbc.co.uk/bbcthree/article/00c38bce-6163-42fa-b7b3-a3f7fce21834

109 G. Clayton, T. Crowther, J. Kerr, S. Sharrock and D. Singer, *Through Her Eyes: Enabling Women's Best Evidence in UK Asylum Appeals*, MRC with Asylum Aid and NatCen, November 2017, p. 8.

110 See R. Cookson and M. Jempson (eds.), *The RAM Report: A Review of the MediaWise Refugees, Asylum-seekers and the Media (RAM) Project, 1999-2005*, MediaWise Trust, 2005; and Article 19, *What's the Story? Results from Research Into Media Coverage of Refugees and Asylum Seekers in the UK*, August 2003 https://www.article19.org/data/files/pdfs/publications/refugees-what-s-the-story-case-study-.pdf

111 Philo, *Bad News for Refugees*, p. 7.

112 Reproduced in the 2003 UN Refugee Agency report *The Changing Face of Protection* http://www.unhcr.org/3f68317d4.pdf

113 See N. Medic, 'How I took on The Sun – and Lost', *The Telegraph*, 15th July 2004 https://www.telegraph.co.uk/news/uknews/1467073/How-I-took-on-The-Sun-and-lost.html

114 Winder, *Bloody Foreigners*, p. 323.

115 Ibid., p. 331.

116 T. Gash, *Criminal: The Truth About Why People Do Bad Things*, Random House, 2016, pp. 172-176, 179-183.

117 See J. Huggler, 'Failed Asylum Seekers Blamed for Rise in Violent Crime in Germany', *Daily Telegraph*, 4th January 2018 https://www.telegraph.co.uk/news/2018/01/04/failed-asylum-seekers-blamed-rise-violent-crime-germany/; and B. Pancevski, 'Teens Roam Streets with Rifles as Crime Swamps Sweden', *The Times*, 21st January 2018 https://www.thetimes.co.uk/article/teens-roam-streets-with-rifles-as-crime-swamps-sweden-q83g055k9

118 D. Blunkett, *The Blunkett Tapes: My Life in the Bear Pit*, Bloomsbury, 2006, p. 276.

119 The video of Brown's gaffe can be accessed at https://www.youtube.com/watch?v=3JZP-W0FAXg

120 Sheppard, *Enoch Powell*, p. 290.

121 See A. Travis, 'Go Home Vans Resulted in 11 People Leaving Britain, Says Report', *The Guardian*, 31st October 2013 https://www.theguardian.com/uk-news/2013/oct/31/go-home-vans-11-leave-britain

122 An excellent summary is provided by M. Broomfield, 'How Theresa May's 'Hostile Environment' Created an Underworld', *New Statesman*, 19th December 2017 https://www.newstatesman.com/2017/12/how-theresa-may-s-hostile-environment-created-underworld

123 Interview with Gawain Towler, 21st November 2017.

124 The full speech can be accessed at https://www.gov.uk/government/speeches/statement-from-the-new-prime-minister-theresa-may

125 N. Bloomer, 'Theresa May's 'Hostile Environment' Turns Doctors Into Border Guards', politics.co.uk, 25th September 2017 http://www.politics.co.uk/comment-analysis/2017/09/25/theresa-may-s-hostile-environment-turns-doctors-into-immigra

126 N. Bloomer and S. Jeraj, 'The Real Theresa May: How the PM Tried to Introduce Immigration Checks in Schools', politics.co.uk, 5th October 2017 http://www.politics.co.uk/comment-analysis/2017/10/05/the-real-theresa-may-how-the-pm-tried-to-introduce-immigrati

127 N. Bloomer, 'Homeless Charities Hit by Fresh Evidence of Links to Home Office', politics.co.uk, 8th March 2017 http://www.politics.co.uk/news/2017/03/08/homeless-charities-hit-by-fresh-evidence-of-links-to-home-of

128 N. Bloomer, 'Woman Reports Rape to Police – and is Arrested on Immigration Charges', politics.co.uk, 28th November 2017 http://www.politics.co.uk/news/2017/11/28/woman-reports-rape-to-police-and-is-arrested-on-immigration

129 N. Bloomer and S. Jeraj, 'Revealed: MPs Using Immigration Enforcement Hotline to Report People to the Home Office', politics.co.uk, 1ˢᵗ September 2017 http://www.politics.co.uk/news/2017/09/01/mps-using-hotline-to-report-immigrants-to-home-office

130 https://www.theguardian.com/uk-news/2018/mar/30/antiguan-who-has-lived-59-years-in-britain-told-he-is-in-uk-illegally

131 See R. Hargrave, 'The Home Office Should Retire the Hostile Environment Approach to Immigration', *Public Finance*, 18ᵗʰ April 2018 https://www.publicfinance.co.uk/opinion/2018/04/home-office-should-retire-hostile-environment-approach-immigration

132 All data from the House of Commons Library briefing into immigration detention.

133 M. Bulman, 'More Than £500m Spent on UK Immigration Detention Over Four Years', *Independent*, 5ᵗʰ February 2018 http://www.independent.co.uk/news/uk/home-news/uk-immigration-detention-centre-cost-taxpayer-brexit-eu-migrants-a8195251.html

134 Dugan, *Finding Home*, p. 235.

135 K. Osamor, 'I'm an MP and I Visited an Immigration Detention Centre Undercover – What I Discovered Was Shocking', *The Independent*, 9ᵗʰ December 2017 http://www.independent.co.uk/voices/home-office-detention-centres-immigration-torture-abuse-deportation-risk-a8101036.html

136 B. Gelbium, '"The Trauma Will Stay With Me Forever" – What's It's Like to be Locked Up Indefinitely by the UK', The London Economic, June 24ᵗʰ 2017 https://www.thelondoneconomic.com/must-reads/trauma-will-stay-forever-like-refugee-locked-indefinitely-uk/24/06/

137 See https://www.inquest.org.uk/deaths-of-immigration-detainees

138 See A. Holt, 'What I Saw When I Went Undercover', BBC, 4ᵗʰ December 2017 http://www.bbc.co.uk/news/resources/idt-sh/g4s_brook_house_immigration_removal_centre_undercover

139 In A. Payne and T. Swift (eds.), *Tactical Reading: A Snappy Guide to the Snap General Election 2017*, Squint Books, 2017, p. 34.

140 S. J. Silverman, *Briefing: Immigration Detention in the UK*, 2ⁿᵈ May 2017 http://www.migrationobservatory.ox.ac.uk/resources/briefings/immigration-detention-in-the-uk/

141 The text of Cooper's speech can be accessed at https://labourlist.org/2014/04/yvette-coopers-immigration-speech-full-text/; see also T. Bale, *Five Year Mission: The Labour Party Under Ed Miliband*, Oxford University Press, 2015, pp. 161-162.

142 P. Bartolo and L. Tilotta (trans. C. Jiang), *Lampedusa: Gateway to Europe*, MacLehose Press, 2016, p. 144.

143 Unsigned article, 'Travelling in Hope', *The Economist*, 22nd October 2016 https://www.economist.com/news/international/21709019-flow-africans-libya-italy-now-europes-worst-migration-crisis-travelling

144 In P. Kingsley, *The New Odyssey: The Story of Europe's Refugee Crisis*, Guardian Books, 2016, p. 259.

145 All data on migrant deaths is from the International Organization for Migration https://missingmigrants.iom.int/

146 Interview with Zoe Gardner, 7th February 2018.

147 Bartolo and Tilotta, *Lampedusa*, p. 59.

148 W. Steavenson, *Circling the Square: Stories from the Egyptian Revolution*, Ecco, 2015, pp. 74-75.

149 R. Goldman, 'What it Means When Five Million Syrians Leave Their Country' , *New York Times*, March 30th 2017 https://www.nytimes.com/2017/03/30/world/middleeast/a-quarter-of-syrias-population-has-fled-what-does-that-look-like.html

150 Kingsley, *The New Odyssey*, p. 76.

151 Ibid., 259.

152 See T. Gillespie and J. Hale, 'What was the Calais 'Jungle'?', *The Sun*, 24th October 2017 https://www.thesun.co.uk/news/1697984/calais-jungle-camp-migrant-refugee-demolished/

153 S. Webb, 'Calais Refugee Crisis: Ferry Services in Chaos After Ship at Port is Stormed by Migrants', *The Mirror*, 23rd January 2016 https://www.mirror.co.uk/news/uk-news/calais-refugee-crisis-ferry-services-7234571

154 Quoted in J. Rutter and R. Carter, *National Conversation on Immigration: Interim Report*, British Future and Hope Not Hate, January 2018, p. 16 http://nationalconversation.uk/wp-content/uploads/2018/01/national-conversation-interim-report-2018-01-v4.pdf

155 J. Robinson, 'Is a 13ft Wall REALLY Going To Stop All of these People Reaching Britain?', *Daily Mail*, 8th September 2016  http://www.dailymail.co.uk/news/article-3779643/Is-13ft-wall-REALLY-going-stop-people-reaching-Britain-New-images-Jungle-reveal-huge-growing-scale-Calais-migrant-problem.html

156 See M. Bulman, 'Dubs Amendment: Child Refugees 'Put In More Danger' As Court Backs Government's Refusal To Take In More Unaccompanied Minors', *The Independent*, 2nd November 2017 http://www.independent.co.uk/news/uk/home-news/dubs-amendment-child-refugees-danger-help-government-refusal-take-more-home-office-court-ruling-a8032986.html

157 Interview with Gardner.

158 A. Suleiman and K. van Dijken, 'Sudan: The EU Partner in Migration Crime', Refugees Deeply, 19th January 2018 https://www.newsdeeply.com/refugees/articles/2018/01/19/sudan-the-e-u-s-partner-in-migration-crime

159 Chandler was speaking in parliament in May 2018, addressing the all party group on refugees.

160 M. Peel, H. Saleh and J. Politi, 'Efforts To Curb Migrant Flows From Libya Under Scrutiny', *Financial Times*, 8th September 2017 https://www.ft.com/content/3e79a7a8-9493-11e7-a9e6-11d2f0ebb7f0

161 Bartolo and Tilotta, *Lampedusa*, p. 151.

162 See E. Colette, 'The Paradox of the EU-Turkey Deal', March 2016 https://www.migrationpolicy.org/news/paradox-eu-turkey-refugee-deal

163 Interview with Gardner.

164 The data is from the UN Refugee Agency, highlighted in a series of graphs tweeted by Italy-based migration researcher Mattio Villa https://twitter.com/emmevilla/status/1006206086381228032

165 The six hundred men, women and children on board the *Aquarius* were eventually diverted to Spain, where the government had agreed to take them in. See K. Snowdon, 'Aquarius Aid Convoy Carrying 630 Migrants Arrive in Spain After a Week Sea,' Huffington Post, 17th June 2018 https://www.huffingtonpost.co.uk/entry/aquarius-migrants-arrive-spain-valencia_uk_5b2629fce4b0783ae129dcb9

166 See O. Jones, 'The EU's Leaders are All Smiles, but Refugees Will Continue To Drown', *The Guardian* 29th June 2018 https://www.theguardian.com/commentisfree/2018/jun/29/angela-merkel-refugee-crisis-drown

167 Reproduced in the 2015 International Journal of Communication report *Understanding the Images of Alan Kurdi with 'Small Data'* http://ijoc.org/index.php/ijoc/article/view/7252

168 M. Bolton, *How To Resist: Turn Protest To Power*, Bloomsbury, 2017, p. 126.

169 See 'Has Britain Become More Welcoming To Refugees?', 8th September 2015 http://ukpollingreport.co.uk/blog/archives/9472

170 P. Wintour, 'UK To Take Up To 20,000 Syrian Refugees Over Five Years, David Cameron Confirms', *The Guardian*, 7th September 2015 https://www.theguardian.com/world/2015/sep/07/uk-will-accept-up-to-20000-syrian-refugees-david-cameron-confirms

171 R. Hargrave, 'The Government is Betraying the 20,000 Refugees It Pledged To Help', politics.co.uk, 20th October 2016 http://www.politics.co.uk/comment-analysis/2016/10/20/the-government-is-betraying-the-20-000-syrian-refugees-it-pl

172 See 'UK Could Extend Target To Rehouse 20,000 Syrian Refugees', BBC, 22nd February 2018  http://www.bbc.co.uk/news/uk-43157002

173 Murray, *Strange Death of Europe*, p. 82.

174 See Ford and Lymperopoulou, 'Immigration: How attitudes in the UK compare with Europe'.

175 See R. Hargrave, *Dividing Lines: Asylum, the Media and Some Reasons for (Cautious) Optimism*, Asylum Aid, 2014 https://www.asylumaid.org.uk/wp-content/uploads/2014/01/DividingLines_V3_highres.pdf

176 S. Katwala, S. Ballinger and M. Rhodes, *How To Talk About Immigration*, British Future, 2014,  p. 10.

177 Ibid., pp. 11-12.

178 Murray, *Strange Death of Europe*, p. 2.

179 Reproduced under a Creative Commons License. Image courtesy of Tim & Selena Middleton https://www.flickr.com/photos/tim_and_selena/4741472722/in/photolist-6jYeUS-ftkyn7-fhpXSe-7buqmj-wfGTa-iqX43j-6kdRSs-6jTZJZ-6jY8P1-6jY-9cy-6jY79Q-6jTUuz-6jYg6w-6jU5j4-6jU2Zv-6jTZk2-6jTXpn-eeK8ut-6jYa6o-5RAchG-am6p6g-Nmf7ts-qBU6FJ-tPGEB-6jU5pK-21bckM3-ySbV4x-UitosN-vNV8g-6jTSy2-6jU49e-6jU1Lz-6jY5Nu-v16gYT-CBTh9F-FRCH8r-8dZhDG-6jU2CH

180 M. Thompson, *Enough Said: What's Gone Wrong With the Language of Politics?* Random House, 2016, pp. 131-133.

181 See F. Luntz, *Words That Work: It's Not What You Say, It's What People Hear*, Hyperion, 2007, p. xiii.

182 Dugan, *Finding Home*, p. 259.

183 Interview with Towler.

184 See the All Party Group on Migration report *Brexit: Beyond the Highly-Skilled – The Needs of Other Economic Stakeholders*, September 2017 http://appgmigration.org.uk/wp-content/uploads/2017/09/APPG-on-Migration-Brexit_Beyond-the-highly-skilled-report-Sept-2017.pdf

185 M. Ruhs and C. Vargas-Silva, *Briefing: The Labour Market Effects of Immigration*, 22nd May 2016 http://www.bbc.co.uk/news/uk-politics-43405680

186 L. Elliott, 'EU migrants have no negative affect on UK wages, says LSE', *The Guardian*, 11th May 2016 https://www.theguardian.com/money/2016/may/11/eu-migrants-had-no-negative-effect-on-uk-wages-says-lse

187 An excellent review of the Kosovar refugee process is provided in A. Bloch, 'Kosovan Refugees in the UK: The Rolls Royce or Rickshaw' in *Forced Migration Review*, August 1999 http://www.fmreview.org/sites/fmr/files/FMRdownloads/en/kosovo/bloch.pdf

188 A. Campbell, *Power and Responsibility: 1999-2001*, Arrow, 2012, p. 707.

189 Bloch, 'Kosovan Refugees in the UK', p. 5.

190 See J. Zylinski, 'Polish and Proud' in Waltham Forest Echo, 27th April 2018 http://walthamforestecho.co.uk/polish-and-proud/

191 D. Conn, "I Want To Study and Play Sport' – A Young Asylum Seeker in Britain, One Year On', *The Guardian*, 6th December 2017 https://www.theguardian.com/society/2017/dec/06/i-want-to-study-and-play-sport-a-young-asylum-seeker-in-in-britain-one-year-on

192 J. Gest, 'Can the Democratic Party Be White Working Class, Too?', *Prospect*, 3rd April 2017 http://prospect.org/article/can-democratic-party-be-white-working-class-too

193 P. Collier, *Exodus: Immigration and Multiculturalism in the 21st Century*, Allen Lane, 2013, pp. 27-53.

194 K. Fox, *Watching the English: The Hidden Rules of English Behaviour*, Hodder, 2004, p. 17.

195 Interview with Towler.

196 J. Wildman, M. Waqas, N. Braakmaan, 'What Immigrants in Britain Think of Immigration', The Conversation, 3rd May 2017 https://theconversation.com/what-immigrants-in-britain-think-of-immigration-75877

# ACKNOWLEDGMENTS

If you tell someone you are writing a book about immigration, the chances are they will share their opinions with you. Several people warned me about the perils of fake news (and very wise they were too). One friend of a friend, sitting with me in a café, took up a napkin and pen and sketched out a theory of progressive voting patterns. A writer thrives on ideas, and I am lucky to be surrounded by people who hold lots of them.

Specific thanks go to Pauline Bock, Zoe Gardner and Gawain Towler, who agreed to interviews for this book. Their opinions, expertise and experience were invaluable.

Dr Todd Swift and Renae Prince at Eyewear were a source of inspiration and practical advice, exactly what someone needs in their editors as they embark on their first book. It is much appreciated.

I also owe a substantial debt to the bosses, editors and friends – the categories overlap, of course – who have indulged my obsession with immigration over the last ten years: Vidhya Alakeson, Molly Anders, Ben Austin, Steve Ballinger, Nicola Boyce, Faye Clark, Dan Corry, James Cracknell, Madeleine Davies, Ian Dunt, Tim Farron, Tim Finch, Helen Fleming, Nabeelah Jaffer, Angela Kail, Sunder

Katwala, Genevieve Maitland Hudson, Katie Nguyen, Rosie Olliver, Matt Rhodes, Alan White, Jenny Willott, Maurice Wren.

Angela and Nabeelah commented on an early draft of this book, and their suggestions were extremely helpful. Thanks both.

*This book is for my family: Ingrid, who has offered wise counsel throughout; and Molly the greyhound, who joined me on some very good walks.*

## OUR OTHER TITLES IN THE SQUINT SERIES

Squint Books focus on the 21st Century Digital Age, from Pop Culture to Politics, Art to Science, with an emphasis on Key Figures

**WWW.EYEWEARPUBLISHING.COM**